DUMBARTON OAKS COLLOQUIUM

ON THE HISTORY

OF LANDSCAPE ARCHITECTURE

II

Edited by

NIKOLAUS PEVSNER

THE PICTURESQUE GARDEN AND ITS INFLUENCE OUTSIDE THE BRITISH ISLES

Dumbarton Oaks
Trustees for Harvard University
Washington, District of Columbia
1974

Library of Congress Catalog Card Number 72-93722
Printed in Germany at J.J. Augustin, Glückstadt

To
The Memory
of
CHRISTOPHER HUSSEY
1899–1970

We dedicate this volume to Christopher Hussey, remembering his pioneer role in the investigation and the appreciation of the picturesque movement in English landscape gardening and his kindness and wisdom for whatever cause he chose to work.

The Picturesque came out in 1927, a superb achievement for a young man of twenty-eight. In the forty-five years it has been studied it has kept its freshness and even in factual matters it has not been overtaken.

Christopher Hussey was educated at Eton and Christ Church and was architectural adviser of *Country Life* from 1930–1964. His long articles on country houses, chiefly Georgian, are of exemplary balance.

Whoever has enjoyed Christopher's and wife's hospitality at Scotney Castle, their Early Victorian house designed by Anthony Salvin, will treasure the memory. So will whoever has watched him on committees listening quietly and in the end coming out with a solution which pleased many and was acceptable to all.

NIKOLAUS PEVSNER

v

Contents

vii

The Genesis of the
English Landscape Garden

S. LANG

Gardening, as far as Gardening is an Art, or entitled to that appellation is a deviation from nature; for if the true taste consists, as many hold, in banishing every appearance of Art, or any traces of the footsteps of man, it would then no longer be a Garden.

Reynolds, *Discourses*

The genesis of the English landscape garden has been the topic of many a book or essay,[1] yet various problems remain and many contradictions are unresolved. The theory most prevalent, that the English landscape garden was modelled on paintings by Claude or Gaspard or Salvator Rosa,[2] cannot be reconciled with an assumption of a slow development towards the fully fledged landscape garden. For this reason, an increasing love of nature as expressed by the literati and philosophers cannot have done more than create a favourable climate for the emergence of this new form of garden. The temples, ruins, obelisks, pyramids and other architectural features, which are considered to be of its essence and are thought to derive also from Claude's paintings,[3] precede the true landscape

[1] C. Hussey, *English Gardens and Landscapes, 1700–1750* (London, 1967), is the most recent work, which with his earlier book *The Picturesque* (London, 1927), reprinted with a new bibliography 1967, stands at the beginning of all modern deliberations on the Landscape Garden and is a most perceptive account of the history of English Landscape Gardening, without which this paper could not have been written.

[2] E. W. Manwaring, *Italian Landscapes in Eighteenth Century England* (New York, 1925), 130. Quoting Walpole, the author says: "In all this the imitation of Claude and Gaspard is perfectly evident." J. Thomson in *The Seasons* mentions Claude, but not in connection with gardening—his description of Hagley (Spring, 11. 903–962) as a landscape garden is an insertion first appearing in the 1744 edition. Cf. Manwaring, *op. cit.*, 104 ff. Only in the last quarter of the century did the idea that gardens should be formed in the image of Claude's or other painters' works take root. See A. Grisebach, *Der Garten, eine Geschichte seiner künstlerischen Gestaltung*, (Leipzig, n.d. [1910], 105), who quotes J. Mayer, *Pomona franconica* (Nuremberg, 1776–1801), "Die neue Gartenkunst nahm die Anlage der Gärten den Baumeistern wieder ab und vertraute dies Geschäft den Malern."

[3] But it is not permissible, as Hadfield has done when discussing Kent, to say: "The scene he attempted was not the English scene, but compiled from the works of the painters we have enumerated [Salvator Rosa, Claude, Poussin]. Temples, obelisks, urns and other symbolic objects were provided to furnish the picture in the true Roman manner, gothick and

garden and belong to what Hussey has aptly called its architectural character of the "heroic age of gardens."[4]

There is little need to explain the nature of the landscape garden, yet a definition will throw some light on the problem in hand. The Oxford English Dictionary was not very forthcoming; they only say "landscape gardening, [is] the art of laying out grounds so as to produce the effect of natural scenery." Their quotations are all rather late; the earliest cited is the title of Humphry Repton's book, *Observations on the Theory and Practice of Landscape Gardening*, of 1805, but the term had already been used by Repton in his *Sketches and Hints on Landscape Gardening* published in 1794.

The term seems actually to have been coined by Shenstone, so at least Spence reports—probably in 1759.[5] By 1753 we have a satirical description. In the copy of April 12 of *The World* one can read this description of a garden: "At your first entrance the eye is saluted by a yellow serpentine river, stagnating through a beautiful valley, which extends nearly twenty yards in length. Over the river is thrown a bridge partly in the Chinese manner and a little ship with sails spread and streamers flying floats in the midst of it. When you have passed this bridge you enter into a grove perplexed with crooked walks."[6] Then follows a description of a hermitage and a temple dedicated to Venus.

Professor Pevsner's definition may be helpful: "The English garden ... is asymmetrical, informal, varied and made of such parts as the serpentine lake, the winding drive and winding path, the trees grouped

---

features of chinoiserie were shortly added to give even fuller value." M. Hadfield, *A History of British Gardening* (London, n.d.), 196. Nor can it be said that "One of the first principles of the Landscape Garden is that of association. Prospects were made not for the eye alone, but to excite the imagination. Here at *Chiswick* are associations enough. 'Every acre,' as *Horace Walpole* said of Stowe, 'brings to one's mind some instance of the parts or pedantry of the taste or want of taste, of the ambition or love of fame, or greatness or miscarriages of those who have inhabited decorated planned or visited the place.'" H. F. Clark, "Lord Burlington's Bijou," *Architectural Review*, 95 (1944), 125. This passage proves clearly that at least one writer on landscape gardening took a later interpretation as an explanation of its origin. No such explanations or deliberations of association exist during the early period. Cf. Manwaring, *op. cit.*, 136.

[4] Hussey, *English Gardens*, 132 and *passim*.

[5] J. Spence, *Anecdotes of Pope*, ed. J. M. Osborn, I (Oxford, 1966), 252, § 606. I. W. V. Chase, *Horace Walpole: Gardenist* (Princeton, 1943), 147, quotes W. Shenstone, *Works*, II (written 1759, first printed 1764), 4th ed. (London, 1773), 54, saying: "... he is credited with having been the first to use the term *landscape* as applied to garden design."

[6] Attention to this magazine was first drawn by K. Clark, *The Gothic Revival* (Oxford, 1928), 51 ff., 62.

in clumps and smooth lawn (mown or cropped by sheep) reaching right up to the French windows of the house."[7]

Thus a landscape garden is not just a garden with crooked walks or little rills,[8] but one with open fields, clumps of trees, wide glades leading up to the house. Brown's gardens looked rather shaven, later ones more luscious, but the principle remained the same. Garden structures are essential, partly hidden behind trees, often of exotic derivation. Flowering shrubs might occur, but no flowers, certainly no parterres or flower beds.

While the Oxford English Dictionary is somewhat reticent on the landscape garden, the entry for the term "landscape" yields, amongst others, ten or so meanings which are of some interest; several identify "landscape" with prospect, e.g., "A view or prospect of natural inland scenery such as can be taken in at a glance from one point of view," or in an obsolete or figurative sense, "a view, prospect of something, a distant prospect, a vista." The stress on prospect or vista is notable. This concept goes back at least to Norgate who in 1650 gives this definition in his *Miniatura:* "Now Landscape, or shape of Land, is but the same with the Latin *Rus, Regiones, Regioncula* and the French *Paisage* or Italian *Paese* and is nothing but a picture of gle belle Vedute, or beautiful prospects of Fields, Cities, Rivers, Castles, Mountaines, Trees or whatsoever delightfull view the Eye takes pleasure in, nothing more in Art or Nature affording soe great variety and beautie as beholding the farre distant Mountaines and strange scituation of ancient Castles mounted on almost inaccessible Rocks, ..."[9]

Nourse, at the end of the century, is also much concerned with the prospect and describes the approach to the country house thus: "But in case it may be thought that such walks or Glades through Woods might hinder the View and Prospect of the House, the Avenue or Approach may be cast into a Figure something resembling a Theatre."[10]

More than half a century later, when the landscape garden was established, Spence reports that Phillip Southcote had made this demand: "There should be Leading Trees or Clumps of Trees to help

[7] N. Pevsner, *The Englishness of English Art,* Penguin ed. (London, 1964), 174.

[8] Switzer's, Bridgeman's and Langley's cannot therefore be called landscape gardens.

[9] E. Norgate, *Miniatura* (1648–1650), ed. M. Hardie (Oxford, 1919), 43.

[10] T. Nourse, *Campania Foelix, an Essay of a Country House* (London, 1700), 302. Nourse possibly was thinking of trees set like wings along a glade. The importance of this will emerge later on. See below, p. 23.

the eye to any more distant Clump, Building, or View."[11] Other
examples exist which have been neglected. One famous example is
Sanderson Miller's Gothic Folly, which was to make an "object from
the House."[12] Shenstone defined a "prospect" as distant images.[13]
Thus, discussions of the period centered on prospects and directed
views, and there were no early references to the picturesque or to
panoramic landscape paintings. Indeed, nobody before Walpole, it
appears, mentions Claude in connection with gardening.[14]

It is true, that later on we do find quotations from Claude in actual
gardens. The most famous one is Stourhead of ca. 1754. But they are
never more than quotations, and, in fact, it seems doubtful whether
there was a direct transference here. More about this later.

There are several more objections to the theory of an influence of
Claude and Gaspard. First, there is what one might call the psychological difficulties of transforming a two-dimensional painting, into a
three-dimensional actual landscape.

The psychological aspect of the laying out of landscape gardens
merits further investigation: the question is, how does a gardener
actually lay out a landscape garden that has to be planned in the
three dimensions of an open landscape, often on an uneven ground,
over hills and dales. An architect works from a definite ground plan
and can and does relate his elevations to it, if he does not make
detailed drawings and models from which to work. The gardener has
hardly any such props; a plan would be of little help, a bird's eye
view of the whole most difficult to achieve. Kent did make such drawings for part of his gardens, but that was much later. By and large,
the gardener must work it all out in his mind. His imagination must
be of a twofold kind; he has to invent his composition—as also every
other artist of course must but he needs a special imagination to carry
his ideas into execution. All this sounds rather elementary; Lancelot
Brown's statement about the "capability" of a stretch of land to be
transformed into a landscape garden makes sense if one takes this

[11] Spence, *Anecdotes*, I, 252.
[12] Hussey, *Picturesque*, 196f.
[13] W. Shenstone, *Works*, 4th ed., II (London, 1773), 114.
[14] See supra, n. 2, and H. Walpole, *Anecdotes of Painting in England*, III (London, 1889),
85 n. 2.Yet the link with painting was not entirely a *post factum* invention. Writers on gardens
were much preoccupied with arrangement of tints and colours, light and shade, perspective
and perspectival tricks, but only relating to single features. The first to talk about colours was
Henry Wotton, who praised Sir Henry Fanshaw's taste in that respect (see p. 9).

difficulty into account. "Capability" Brown obviously must have looked at an existing landscape and decided from the lie of the land which features to stress, where to plant his trees, where to clear a wood.

Sir William Temple of *Sharawadgi* fame had warned would-be layers-out of "irregular" gardens how difficult such a task might prove to be: "But I should hardly advise any of these attempts in the figure of gardens among us; they are adventures of too hard achievement for any common hands; and though there may be more honour if they succeed well, yet there is more dishonour if they fail, and it is twenty to one they will; whereas in regular figures it is hard to make any great and remarkable faults."[15]

A second objection to the theory of the influence of Claude's painting concerns the date of the origins of the landscape garden. If Claude's painting was important, why was its influence not felt earlier? The reason given is that only ca. 1700 and in the following two decades did love of unbridled landscape, expressed by Pope and Addison, etc., stimulate the gardeners to move away from the stiff Dutch formal garden.

Yet the elements of landscape garden design had been discussed in earlier literature. Descriptions of natural or irregular gardens appeared as early as 1685, and concepts of variety and contrast as elements of design were prevalent in the seventeenth century. It was Sir William Temple who preceded Pope and Addison in his *Garden of Epicurus*, published in 1685, with his statement about the Chinese garden and *Sharawadgi*.[16] He also described an existing garden in terms of, if not a landscape garden, then at least an irregular and "natural" garden:

[15] W. Temple, *Upon the Garden of Epicurus; or of Gardening, in the Year 1685*, Works, III (London, 1770), 230.

[16] ... for there may be other Forms [of gardens] wholly irregular, that may, for ought I know, have more beauty than any of the others; but they must owe it to ... some great Race of Fancy or Judgment in the contrivance.... Something of this I have seen in some Places, but heard more of it from others, who have lived much among the *Chinese;* a People whose way of Thinking seems to lie as wide of ours in *Europe,* as their Country does .... But their greatest reach of Imagination is employed in contriving Figures, where the Beauty shall be great and strike the Eye, but without any Order or Disposition of Parts, that shall be commonly or easily observ'd. And though we have hardly any Notion of this sort of Beauty, yet they have a particular Word to express it; and where they find it hit their Eye at first sight, they say the *Sharawadgi* is fine or is admirable, or any such expression of Esteem...." (*Ibid.,* 186). See also S. Lang and N. Pevsner, "A Note on Sharawaggi," *Architectural Review,* 106 (1949), reprinted in N. Pevsner, *Studies in Art, Architecture and Design,* I (London, 1968), 102–106.

"a garden the other side of the house, which is all of that sort, very wild, shady and adorned with rough rock work and fountains."

Also to the end of the seventeenth century belongs Timothy Nourse. In his book on the country house he demanded that an estate should be built on a gently rising ground in open country, preferably with a river in the distance, the open prospect terminated by other hills. His garden consisted of three parts, each on a separate terrace. The first two were to be traditionally formal in design, though full of surprises and "variety" but the third and highest was to be of a totally different character. There the evergreens were to be planted in "some negligent Order," and "up and down let there be little Banks or Hillocks, planted with wild Thyme, Violets, Primroses, Cowslips, Daffadille, Lillies of the Valley, Blew-Bottles, Daisies, with all kinds of Flowers which grow wild in the Fields and Woods." This third garden "should be made to represent a perpetual Spring .... In a word, let this Third Region or Wilderness be Natural-Artificial; that is, let all things be dispos'd with that cunning, as to deceive us into a belief of a real Wilderness or Thicket." And outside the garden "let there be planted Walks of Trees to adorn the Landskip ... and thus at length the Prospect may terminate on Mountains, Woods, or such Views as the Situation will admit of."[17] Nourse was the first to go outside the garden and to suggest organizing the actual landscape.

[17] Nourse, *Campania Foelix*, 319 ff. A "wilderness" according to the Oxford English Dictionary is "a piece of ground in a large garden or park, planted with trees, and laid out in an ornamental or fantastic style, often in the form of a maze or labyrinth." They quote Dryden's *Evening Love* V (of 1668), "Disperse yourselves, some into the Wilderness, some into the Allies, and some into the Parterre." and also, H. Chamberlain in his *History and Survey of London* (London, 1770): "In one part of it [sc. the park] is a pretty wilderness laid out in walks, and planted with a variety of evergreen trees." L. Meager includes in the title of *The English Gardener* (London, 1670) a description of a chapter on "The ordering of the Garden of Pleasure, with variety of Knots, and Wilderness—work after the best fashion, all Cut in Copper Plates, etc. ..." None of the plans are of other than "Knots". There is one "Wilderness Work" and one labyrinthian pattern "For a Wilderness"; they have nothing remotely to do with "nature" or landscape.

Nourse demands a real wilderness, that is presumably one which does not just display yet another formal pattern. Such "real" wildernesses could be seen in Italy and are described in classical writings and no doubt these were Nourse's sources. He quotes the "Old Romans" and their activities (p. 299).

Pope's remarks on gardening, as reported by Spence, refer to comparisons with painting. Pope was foremost in promoting in England the word "picturesque" which had recently been imported from France. When he compares gardening with painting he talks a little about colour, but mainly about perspective: in his *Epistle to Burlington* of 1731 he says that "the genius of the landscape joins willing woods, and varies shades from shades, Now breaks, or now directs, th'intending Lines, Paints as you plant, and, as you work, designs." In 1739

There is one frequently repeated conception in these early descriptions, namely the conception of contrast. It was first introduced by Henry Wotton, to whom we also owe the first description of the "natural garden", in 1624.

> First, I must note a certaine contrarietie betweene *building* and *gardening*: For as Fabriques should bee *regular*, so Gardens should bee *irregular*, or at least cast into a very wilde *Regularitie*. To exemplifie my conceit: I have seene a *Garden* (for the maner perchance incomparable) into which the first Accesse was a high walke like a *Tarrace*, from whence might bee taken a generall view of the whole *Plott* below; but rather in a delightfull confusion, then with any plaine distinction of the pieces. From this the *Beholder* descending many steps, was afterwards conveyed againe by severall *mountings* and *valings*, to various entertainements of his *sent*, and *sight*; which I shall not neede to describe (for that were poeticall) let me onely note this, that every one of these diversities was as if hee had been *Magically* transported into a new Garden . . . . hee did so precisely examine the *tinctures* and *seasons* of his flowres, that in their *setting*, the *inwardest* of those which were to come up at the same time, should always be a little *darker* than the *outmost*, and so serve them for a kinde of gentle *shadow*, like a piece not of *Nature*, but of *Arte*. . . .[18]

Could this "pictorial" description have inspired Pope's sayings: "All gardening is landscape-painting. Just like a landscape hung up," or "you may distance things by darkening them."[19]

The idea of a visitor "being magically transported" from one view to another need not be Wotton's own. He could have read such a description, albeit not of a garden walk but of a city street, in Alberti's *De Re Aedificatoria* where he advocates a winding street to create

---

he said to Spence that: "The lights and shades in gardening are managed by disposing the thick grove-work, the thin, and the openings in a proper manner of which the eye generally is the properest judge." (Spence, *Anecdotes*, I, 253 § 611).

[18] H. Wotton, *The Elements of Architecture*, Facs. Reprint of 1st Ed. (London, 1624) Introd. by F. Hard, published for the Folger Shakespeare Library (Charlottesville, 1968), 109f.

[19] Spence, *Anecdotes*, I, 252 § 606; 253 § 610.

variety.[20] Alberti considers variety, Wotton's "contrarietie" one of the most important concepts contributing to the good looks of a building or an object.

Indeed, the concept of variety goes back to Aristotle and was a consistent element in the aesthetics of seventeenth century England. Nearer to the period under discussion is Norgate, who was quoted before as a writer for whom landscape affords the greatest variety in Art or Nature.[21] He is followed by Peacham in 1612: "*Varietie*, is various and the rules of it so difficult that to define or describe it, were as to draw one picture which should resemble all the faces in the world...." Robert Boyle can be quoted as having said, "Varietie is a thing so pleasing to humane Nature, that there are many things which it recommends to us." Louis Le Roy, who was translated into English in 1594, points out that the world order is "maintained by contraries," adding that "... nature is so desirous of contraries, making of them, all decency, and beauty...."

Another tradition is that of Christian optimism for which Hooker (1594) can be quoted: "Abundance [of God] doth show itself in variety," and Thomas Johnson's translation of *The Works of that Famous Chirurgian Ambrose Parry* (1634), "... so we may behold the superficies of this earth clothed with an almost infinite variety of trees, shrubs and herbs...the innumerable diversities of roots, leaves, flowers, etc., etc."

Henry Wotton appears to have been instrumental in creating a new literary genre, that of garden literature, based less on a real feeling for nature than on traditional conceptions going back ultimately to ideas of retirement, possibly to notions of primitivism and very largely resting on ideas of variety and contrast.[22] Thus the writings on gardening of Pope and Addison, the apparent protagonists of natural gardening, also must stem principally from this literary tradition.

With this literary tradition in mind, let us now examine the writings and gardens of Pope and Addison. The importance of this tradition

[20] L. B. Alberti, *De Re Aedificatoria*, IV, v

[21] "Designe or drawing hath, according to Giorgio Vassari, Accident or chance for its father .... His words are: Credono alcuni che il padre del Designo fusso il caso ...." (E. Norgate, *Miniatura*, 79). The following outline and its quotations are taken from H. V. S. Ogden, "Variety and Contrast in Seventeenth Century Aesthetics," *Journal of the History of Ideas*, 10 (1949) 159–182.

[22] This "garden literature" is reminiscent of the Country House Poem described by G. R. Hibbard in "The Country House Poem of the Seventeenth Century," *Journal of the Warburg and Courtauld Institutes*, 19 (1956), 159–174.

to Pope is clear in his *Guardian* essay of 1713, where he mentions, *expressis verbis*, the attitude of the ancients towards nature and compares it with that of the modern, of course to the detriment of the latter. When he makes fun of topiary works, he points out that the "citizen," possibly the upstarts, in fact the "lower orders," fall for it, those who are uneducated and unlettered. Is it possible that Pope was thinking of the newly arrived Dutch?

The concepts of contrast and variety also appear prominently in Pope's writings and deliberations on gardening. That he had read Wotton could have been assumed even if we had not actual proof.[23] There are other sources as well. A few of Pope's several references to variety and contrast (which were all reported by Spence in his *Anecdotes*) can be quoted. Spence asked Pope, "Should not variety be one of the rules?" Pope replies, "Certainly, one of the chief, but that is included mostly in the contrasts . . ."[24] Pope's disdain for the prevailing garden designs is directed against the lack of contrast more than against their artificiality.

In his description of Windsor Forest, Pope makes something like a theoretical statement on aesthetics, albeit not a new one.

> Where Order in Variety we see,
> And where, tho' all things differ, all agree.[25]

This statement goes well with one he made in a discussion with Southcote which again Spence reports: "Mr. Pope used to say that all the beauties of gardening might be comprehended in one word, variety." "Why so they may," was Southcote's reply.[26]

Pope criticized Lord Bathurst who "should have raised two or three mounts because his situation is all a plain, and nothing can please without variety." One cannot help feeling that Pope went rather out of his way in these passages to introduce variety.[27]

Yet despite his championing of the concepts of contrast and variety, he appears not to have carried these ideas into actual practice. His

---

[23] Spence, *Anecdotes*, I, 225, § 617.
[24] Spence, *Anecdotes*, I, 254, § 612.
[25] *Windsor Forest* (1712), ll. 17–18.
[26] Spence, *Anecdotes*, I, 251, § 604.
[27] Spence quotes a number of other statements by Pope relating to gardens: Spence, *op. cit.*, I, 249–257.

garden, which has been hailed as a landscape garden,[28] at best in its
final form of 1745 only approximates one.[29] By that time true landscape gardens were in existence that went far beyond Pope's garden.
Furthermore, there is no proof that the plan of 1745 (Fig. 1) represents
his first endeavour of 1718, or of 1722–25, since it is known that Pope
carried out many alterations as he or his gardeners went along.[30] The

[28] The literature on this garden is profuse; practically every book on the Landscape Garden
refers to it. See amongst others, M. Mack, *The Garden and the City* (Toronto, 1969), 21, who
says: "Despite the reputation of Pope's garden with his friends and contemporaries, we have
surprisingly little detailed information about it, still less about what it meant to him." When
Pope described this garden he appears to do so in terms of a landscape garden, stressing
the "romantic" views, wild winding walks, talking of a part of the garden as "inexpressibly
awful and solemn", and of the "solemnity of the scene." He mentions repeatedly the ruins
contained in it and ends by suggesting that "a little temple [be] built on a neighbouring
round hill that is seen from all points of the garden and extremely pretty. It would finish
some walks, and particularly be a fine termination to the river to be seen from the entrance
into that deep scene I have described by the cascade, where it would appear as in the clouds,
between the tops of some lofty trees that form an arch before it . . . ." [quoted by M. Hadfield,
A History of British Gardening (London, n.d.), 188 ff.] Mack, *op. cit.*, 56, quotes a description
of Pope's garden from the mid-forties: "These Wilderness-Groves are either Quincunces, or
cut thro' by many narrow serpentine Walks; and as we recede from the Boundary and
approach towards the Center, the Scene opens and becomes less entangled; the Alleys widen,
the Walks grow broader, and either terminate in small green Plots of the finest Turf, or lead
to the Shell Temple. The Middle of the Garden approaches nearest to a Lawn or open
Green, but is delightfully diversified with Banks and Hillocks; which are entirely cover'd
with Thickets of Lawrel, Bay, Holly, and many other Evergreens and Shrubs, rising one
above another in beautiful Slopes and Intermixtures, where Nature freely lays forth the
Branches, and disports uncontroul'd; except what may be entirely prun'd away for more
Decency and Convenience to the surrounding Grass-plots, for no Shear-work or Tonsure is
to be found in all the Scene. Towards the South side of the Garden is a Plantation of Vines
curiously disposed and dress'd; it adjoins the Wilderness, and is in the same Taste, but opener
to the Sun, and with more numerous interveening Paths. Among the Hillocks on the upper
Part of the open Area, rises a Mount much higher than the rest, and is composed of more
rude and indigested Materials; it is covered with Bushes and Trees of a wilder Growth, and
more confused Order, rising as it were out of Clefts of Rocks, and Heaps of rugged and
mossy Stones; among which a narrow intricate Path leads in an irregular Spiral to the Top;
where is placed a Forest Seat or Chair, that may hold three or four Persons at once, over-
shadowed with the Branches of a spreading Tree. From this Seat we face the Temple, and
overlook the various Distribution of the Thickets, Grass-plots, Alleys, Banks, etc. Near this
Mount lies the broadest Walk of the Garden, leading from the Center to the uppermost
Verge; where, upon the gentle Eminence of a green Bank, stands an *Obelisk*, erected by
Mr. *Pope* to the Memory of his Mother.... As this Obelisk terminates the longest Prospect
of Mr. *Pope's* Garden, it shall also put a Period to my Description; which is not of a Place
that bears the high Air of State and Grandeur, that surprizes you with the vastness of Expence
and Magnificence; but an elegant Retreat of a Poet strongly inspired with the Love of Nature
and Retirement; and shews you, with respect to these Works, what was the Taste of the
finest Genius that this or any other Age has produced." *Newcastle General Magazine*, I (January,
1748), 27–28.

[29] The plan was first shown in J. Serle, *A Plan of Mr. Pope's Garden* (London, 1745).

[30] Pope made several designs for his garden on the backs of his Homer translation (British
Museum, MS. Add. 4807–9); these were first mentioned by N. Ault, *New Light on Pope*,

plan of 1745 bears a considerable likeness to the sixteenth century Italian garden, Pratolino, the plan of which had been published two years previously, and also to plans published by Switzer (Fig. 21) and Batty Langley in the 1720's.[31]

When Pope began his garden he made a revealing remark: "Gardening is ... nearer God's own Work, than Poetry."[32] It is perhaps less important that gardening wins over poetry than that such a comparison is made at all.[33] This *paragone* is of more consequence for an explanation of the landscape garden than most of Pope's other statements.

First, however, a word about Addison. He was also a gardener. Much has been made of his garden activities. He himself talks of his little rill, which he lets "run in the same manner as it would do in an open field so that it generally passes through banks of violets and primroses, plots of willow or other plants that seem to be of its own producing."[34] Evidently, there were "natural" features like flowers and feathered trees, but whatever Addison thought his garden was, it certainly was not a landscape garden. It was obviously not a naked

---

ch. 5, "Mr. Alexander Pope, Painter," (London, 1949) 68–100, 74f. Two of these designs were recently published and discussed by A. J. Sambrook, "The Shape and Size of Pope's Garden," *Eighteenth Century Studies*, 5 (1972), 450–455. He, however, seems to have failed to recognize their true meaning (455).

[31] S. Switzer, *Ichnographia Rustica*, III (London, 1742), pl. 39. B. Langley, *New Principles of Gardening*, (London, 1728), pls. VI, XIV. B. S. Sgrilli, *Descrizione della regia villa, fontane e fabbriche di Pratolino* (Florence, 1742).

[32] Spence, *Anecdotes*, I, 249.

[33] Bacon was possibly the first to make a similar comparison. He begins his essay *Of Gardens* as follows: "God Almighty first planted a garden." Cf. also H.-J. Possin, *Natur und Landschaft bei Addison* (Tübingen, 1965), 45.

[34] The whole passage runs as follows:

"I have several acres about my house, which I call my garden, and which a skilful gardener would not know what to call. It is a confusion of kitchen and parterre, orchard and flower garden, which lie so mixed and interwoven with one another, that of a foreigner, who had seen nothing of our country, should be conveyed into my garden at his first landing, he would look upon it as a natural wilderness, and one of the uncultivated parts of our country ... There is the same irregularity in my plantations, which run into as great a wilderness as their nature will permit. I take in none that do not naturally rejoice in the soil; and am pleased, when I am walking in a labyrinth of my own raising, not to know whether the next tree I shall meet with is an apple, or an oak, an elm, or a pear-tree ... I must not omit, that there is a fountain rising in the upper part of my garden, which forms a little wandering rill, and administers to the pleasure as well as the plenty of the place. I have so conducted it, that it visits most of my plantations; and have taken particular care to let it run in the same manner as it would do in an open field, so that it generally passes through banks of violets and primroses, plots of willow, or other plants, that seem to be of its own producing." (*Spectator*, 477).

Dutch garden; was it perhaps modelled on an Italian or French garden?[35]

Although Addison on his return from France praised the king who "has humored the Genius of the Place,"[37] evidence suggests that his garden was designed in a formal manner. A description of it from the early nineteenth century, not very long after the death of Addison's daughter who continued to live at Bilton, begins thus: "The gardens attached to this mansion are rather extensive, and are yet preserved in all the formality of the old taste. Straight lines, and long and massy hedges of yew, prevail throughout."[36] All that remains at Bilton Grange is a straight avenue of might trees, a lawn, some yew hedges; it all indeed seems quite straight.

There is no need to refer here to Addison's essays on the imagination, but it may again be interesting and useful to point out that Addison too cannot have been unaware of Alberti; the following passage appears to foreshadow Addison's hymn to the imagination, and somehow sounds like a blueprint for the landscape garden:

> But Nature generally offers more Conveniences,... for adorning the situation than the region; for we very frequently meet with circumstance extremealy noble and surprising, such as Promontories, Rooks, broken Hills...high and sharp, grottoes, caverns, springs and the like; near which, if we would have our Situation strike the Beholders with Surprise, we may build to our Heart's desire.

Compare this to Addison's,

> Everything that is new or uncommon raises a pleasure in the imagination, because it fills the soul with an agreeable surprise ...We are, indeed, so often conversant with one set of objects,... that whatever is new or uncommon contributes a

---

[35] The influence of Italian gardens on English ones remains still unexplored, but an investigation becomes now imperative in view of E. MacDougall's "*Ars Hortulorum:* Sixteenth Century Garden Iconography and Literary Theory in Italy," *The Italian Garden*, Dumbarton Oaks Colloquium on the History of Landscape Architecture. I, ed. D. Coffin (Washington, 1972), 37–60.

[36] "The King has humoured the Genius of the place and only made use of so much art as is necessary to Help and regulate Nature without reforming her too much." (cf. *Spectator*, 583). He evidently referred to Fontainebleau; see P. Smithers, *The Life of Joseph Addison*, 2nd ed. (Oxford, 1968), 319. "In France he [Addison] had preferred the carefully studied negligence of Fontainebleau to the magnificent formalism of Versailles."

[37] W. Dugdale and other later authorities, *Warwickshire* (Coventry, 1817), 154.

little to vary human life, and to direct our minds.... Groves, fields, and meadows are at any season of the year pleasant to look upon, but never so much as in the opening of the spring, when they are... not yet too much accustomed and familiar to the eye. For this reason there is nothing that more enlivens a prospect than rivers, jetteaus, or falls of water, where the scene is perpetually shifting, and entertaining the sight every moment with something that is new.[38]

It is possible that Addison's deliberation on the imagination exercized some considerable influence on the arrival of the landscape garden, more than much of the talk about nature.[39] Addison made two more statements of some weight which may help us to solve the problem of the landscape garden. For one he hinted at—and indeed practised—the enclosure of common land. This increasing practice had some influence on the development of the landscape garden, and it may explain the idea that all England was a garden, as well as Switzer's "extensive" gardening. This aspect, already mentioned by Hussey, is still entirely unexplored but might be well worth investigating.[40] Secondly, Addison compared the garden to poetry; we might remember Pope's saying that gardening is nearer to God's own work than poetry.[41] Addison links the two in a more practical way: he says, "There are as many types of poetry as there are of gardening." He compares the parterre makers to epigrammatists and sonneteers, the contrivers of treillages and cascades to romance writers, London and Wise to "heroic" poets. And finally he describes the "irregular garden as being altogether after the Pindaric manner."[42] He could have found

[38] L. B. Alberti, *De Re Aed.*, VI, iv; *Ten Books on Architecture*, tr. G. Leoni, ed. J. Rykwert (London, 1955), 116.

[39] According to G. S. Rousseau, "Science and the Discovery of the Imagination in Enlightened England," *Eighteenth Century Studies*, 3 (1969), 110, "imagination" was discovered precisely in the second half of the seventeenth century. Locke was most important, especially his associationism. Hume, too, talks about imagination.

[40] Switzer, *Ichnographia*, 2nd ed., I (London, 1742), xxxviii and elsewhere, "for extensive" gardening. Cf. Hussey, *English Gardens*, 15f.

[41] Supra p. 13.

[42] Here is the passage which deserves being quoted in full: "I think there are as many kinds of gardening as of poetry; your makers of parterres and flower gardens are epigrammatists and sonneteers in this art; contrivers of bowers and grottoes, treillages and cascades, are romance writers. Wise and London are our heroic poets. As for myself, you will find, by the account which I have already given you, that my compositions in gardening are altogether after the Pindaric manner, and run into the beautiful wildness of nature, without affecting the nicer elegancies of art." *Spectator*, No. 477.

mention of Pindar and a comparison between Pindar and other poets in Rapin's treatise on Aristotle's Poetics.[43] Rapin was a highly influential author in the seventeenth century and particularly well known for his poem on gardening.[44] His *Traité du poème épique*, translated in 1695, was the standard work on heroic poetry.

Addison could have read about divisions of landscape also in Henri Testelin's treatise, *The Sentiment of the Most Excellent Painters Concerning the Practice of Painting*,

> In the disposition of the Ordonnance there are three general parts to be considered, viz. 1. The designing the place with respect to...the disposition of things that ought to serve for the ground-work, whether they be of (1). Landskip, whether /(a)/ Uninhabited places, where we have the liberty of representing all the extravagant effects of Nature, and the confused products of an incultivated Land, in an irregular, but pleasant disposition. Or /(b)/, Inhabited where we ought to describe places of pasture, of cultivated Plants, of Orchards in fruitful and agreeable Appearances; because people commonly seek out pleasant places, and such as are convenient for their dwelling. (2). Building either /a/ Rustique and Country, which we may dispose of in such sort and form as we think best for the Advantage of the figures, and according to the Ideas of the Subjects. /b/. Regular as Architecture, where we may choose its advantages by the difference of its Aspects and Orders.[45]

Above all, Addison could have found such divisions in de Piles' *Cours de Peinture*, published in Paris in 1708. In the English translation of 1743, we read:

> Among the many different styles of landskip, I shall confine myself to two; the heroick and the pastoral or rural; for all other styles are but a mixture of these.

[43] R. Rapin, "On Aristotle's Poesie," in *Critical Works*, II (London, 1706), xix, xxx.

[44] R. Rapin, *Hortorum Libri IV* (Paris, 1665); first translated by John Evelyn Jr., 1673, secondly by J. Gardener, 1700; the second book (on trees) was incorporated by Evelyn into his *Silva*.

[45] Quoted here from Ogden, "Seventeenth Century Aesthetics," 80, n. 19, who reprints the not very clear 1688 translation.

The heroick style is a composition of objects, which, in their kinds draw both from art and nature, everything that is great and extraordinary in either. The situations are perfectly agreeable and surprising. The only buildings are temples, pyramids, antient places of burial, altars consecrated to the divinities, pleasure houses of regular architecture....

The rural style is a representation of countries, rather abandoned to the caprice of nature than cultivated: We there see nature simple, without ornament, and without artifice; but with all those graces with which she adorns herself much more, when let to herself, than when constrained by art...

As a counter balance to heroick landskip, I think it would be proper to put into the pastoral, besides a great character of truth, some affecting extraordinary, but probable effect of nature as was Titian's custom. The chief parts of landskip are, I think, their openings or situations, accidents, skies and clouds, off skips and mountains, verdure or turfing, rocks, grounds or lands, terraces, fabricks, waters, foregrounds, plants, figures and trees:...

Buildings in general are a great ornament in landskip, even when they are Gothick, or appear partly inhabited and partly ruinous; they raise the imagination by the use they are thought to be designed for; as appears from antient towers, which seem to have been the habitations of fairies, and are now retreats for shepheards and owls. Poussin has very elegantly handled the Roman manner of architecture in his works, as Bourdon has done the Gothick; which, however Gothick, fails not to give a sublime air to his landskip.[46]

De Piles then suggests mixing the various brands of landscapes.[47] This fact will prove important later on. The passages just quoted from de Piles seem like a blue print for the landscape garden and what has, somewhat irreverently, been called garden furniture. De Piles might have derived his text from Lomazzo, whose description of various

[46] R. de Piles, *The Principles of Painting* (London, 1743), 124f. This passage, as well as that by Lomazzo, was first quoted by E. H. Gombrich who also established their derivation from Serlio and Vitruvius; see "The Renaissance Theory of Art and the Rise of Landscape," in *Norm and Form* (London, 1966), first published as "Renaissance Artistic Theory and the Development of Landscape Painting," in *Gazette des Beaux Arts*, ser. 6, 41 (1953), 335–360.

[47] *Principles*, 152.

forms of landscape also seems to foreshadow the English landscape garden, however far-fetched such a parallel might appear:

> Those who have shown excellence and grace in this branch of painting, both in private and public places have discovered various ways of setting about—such as fetid, dark under-ground places, religious and macabre, where they represent grave yards, tombs, deserted houses, sinister and lonesome sites, caves, dens, ponds and pools; (secondly) privileged places where they show temples, consistories, tribunals, gymnasiums and schools, (or else) places of fire and blood with furnaces, mills, slaughter houses, gallows and stocks; others bright with serene air, where they represent palaces, princely dwellings, pulpits, theatres, thrones and all the magnificent and regal things; others again places of delight with fountains, fields, gardens, seas, rivers, bathing places and places for dancing.
>
> There is yet another kind of landscape where they represent workshops, schools, inns, market places, terrible deserts, forests, rocks, stones, mountains, woods, ditches, water, rivers, ships, popular meeting places, public baths or rather *terme*.[48]

Lomazzo goes back to Serlio who in his turn echoes Vitruvius:

> There are three kinds of scenes, one called the tragic, second, the comic, third the satyric. Their decorations are different and unlike each other in scheme—Tragic scenes are delineated with columns, pediments, statues, and other objects suited to Kings; comic scenes exhibit private dwellings, with balconies and views representing rows of windows, after the manner of ordinary dwellings; satyric scenes are decorated with trees, caverns, mountains, and other rustic objects delineated in landscape style.[49]

Serlio actually illustrates the three scenes. His treatise was widely distributed in many editions, and his stage sets much imitated, in particular the "satyric" stage which displays a landscape and some

---

[48] G. P. Lomazzo, *Trattato dell'Arte della Pittura, Scultura ed Architettura*, VI, lxii, quoted from E. Gombrich's translation, "Renaissance art and landscape," 120.

[49] Vitruvius, *de Arch*. V, vi, 9. *The Ten Books on Architecture*, tr. M. H. Morgan (New York, 1960), 150.

rustic cottages. Inigo Jones, for one, imitated Serlio in one of his designs for the stage.

De Piles must have commended himself to Addison and Pope and their friends because of his advocacy of, and belief in, surprises and variety; to Addison in particular because of his discussion of imagination.[50]

De Piles' work is, as the title says, primarily concerned with painting, but poetry and poetic theory comes into it as well. Pope had painterly aspirations and must have been interested in art theory:[51] he had sent Du Fresnoy's treatise in Dryden's translation to his teacher Jervas, adding a dedication.[52] Both were interested in the *paragone* of painting and poetry. Pope talks about the "sister arts", and de Piles discusses the poetry versus painting problem at some length.[53] Addison, on the other hand, shows himself well informed on painters, and, at one moment, he says about Boileau, "Amongst all the French critics...," indicating that he knew the lot.[54] He even mentions Vitruvius, and Pope mentions the story of Dinocrates, proving his acquaintance with this writer.[55]

Neither Pope's nor Addison's gardens were true landscape gardens. They might have dispensed with topiary and not been as naked as the Dutch garden, but that was all. Both writers' theoretical statements could be shown to belong to a literary tradition, in parts deriving from artistic theoreticians like Alberti or de Piles. That de Piles's sources were theatrical is of great importance. It so happens that not only Pope had very strong links with the stage, but Addison too, and

[50] There is also a passage in Rapin's "On Aristotle's Poesie," 188, which seems relevant; this passage discusses variety principally, but also heroic poetry and may have thus recommended itself also to the early 18th century literati: "The unity of the Action however Simple and Scrupulous it ought to be, is no Enemy to those Delights which naturally arise from Variety, when the Variety is attended with that Order and that Proportion which makes Uniformity, as one Palace may contain the various Ornaments of Architecture, and a great Diversity of Parts, provided it be Built in the same Order, and after the same Design. This Variety hath a large Field in Heroick Poesie; the Enterprizes of War, the Treatises of Peace, Ambassies, Negotiations, Voyages, Councils, Debates, Building of Palaces and Towns, Manners, Passions, unexpected Discoveries ... may there be employed, so be that all go to the same end."

[51] Cf. N. Ault, *Mr. Alexander Pope, Painter* (London, 1949), 68–84, where he outlines Pope's painterly career and interest.

[52] Ault, *op. cit.*, 71f.

[53] De Piles, *Principles*, 32.

[54] *Spectator*, 592.

[55] Spence, *Anecdotes*, 256, § 618. Spence mentions Dinocrates, and Pope replies in such a way that it is obvious he knows about Vitruvius.

others involved early on in the Landscape Garden like Burlington were deeply committed to the stage.[56] Vanbrugh, too, whatever his status as a landscape gardener is, had been a man of the theatre for some time in his life.[57]

If Pope's and Addison's gardening activity had nothing to do with landscape gardens neither had Burlington's early garden at Chiswick or Vanbrugh's at Claremont and elsewhere. Yet a number of gardens in the first quarter of the eighteenth century have in common one feature that has always been considered as an integral characteristic of the Landscape Garden, namely, the very profuse presence of garden structures. Chiswick, Claremont, Stowe, Cirencester, were all studded with temples, ruins, obelisks, classical seats and Gothic bits and pieces.

The most notable amongst these gardens are Chiswick and Claremont, designed before Kent began work, and the early Stowe. Of these gardens we know something, and of a few others as well. Lord Burlington had had several small temples put in his garden at Chiswick before Kent worked there, and one must assume that the *patte d'oie* was also arranged early on, although not by Kent in 1725 as Hussey has suggested (Figs. 2, 3, 4).[58] *Patte d'oie* arrangements were frequent in seventeenth century gardens in France, and there is one in Hampton Court. Chiswick's, however, was different not only because it was smaller, but because each avenue was terminated by an architectural feature.[59]

[56] Pope's connection with the stage is discussed by M. Goldstein, *Pope and the Augustan Stage* (Stanford, 1958). Addison frequently discusses the theatre and the stage in some detail and was obviously much interested. For Burlington and his role in bringing Italian opera to England see R. Wittkower, "Lord Burlington and William Kent," *Archaeological Journal*, 102 (1947), 152; and more fully, idem., "English Palladianism, the Landscape Garden, China and the Enlightenment," *L'Arte*, ser. 3, 6 (1969), 21.

[57] Vanbrugh had been a playwright and was otherwise involved with the theatre before he became an architect. See L. Whistler, *Sir John Vanbrugh, Architect and Dramatist* (London, 1938), 90–115.

[58] F. Kimball, *Journal of the Royal Institute of British Architects*, Ser. 3, 34 (1927), 675–693; 35 (1927), 14–16. There it is proved conclusively that the garden structures preceded Kent's landscaping activity. Kimball dates most temples between 1717 and 1727 (*op. cit.*, xxxiv, 682f., 691) and fixes the Bagno for 1717, the date which we find in *Vitruvius Britannicus*, III (London, 1725), 26. Cf. R. Wittkower, "Burlington and Kent," 160, who quotes Macky's *Journey through England*, published in 1724.

[59] Macky in 1724 writes that all walks end in little buildings: "The whole contrivance of (the fine Gardens at Chiswick) is the Effect of his Lordship's own Genius, and singular fine Taste; Every Walk terminates with some little Building, one with a Heathen Temple, for instance the Pantheon; another a little Villa, where my Lord often dines instead of his House ... another Walk terminates with a Portico, in imitation of Covent Garden Church." Another *Patte d'oie* similar to Chiswick was in Hartwell House, Buckinghamshire, cf. Hussey, *English Gardens*, fig. 6; and there were others.

Single vistas directed towards a terminal feature occurred also in Vanbrugh's Claremont and in Bridgeman's Stowe (Figs. 5, 6). For Stowe
the 1724 description by Lord Percival makes it clear that garden structures of great variety existed, and that the garden was arranged in
such a manner that the visitor walked from vista to vista and from
prospect to prospect.

> ... It consists of a great number of walks, terminated by sum-
> mer houses, and heathen Temples of different structure,
> and adorned with statues cast from the Anticks. Here you
> see the Temple of Apollo, there a Triumphal Arch. The gar-
> den of Venus is delightful; you see her standing in her
> Temple, at the head of a noble bason of water.... At the
> end of the gravel walk leading from the house, are two hea-
> then Temples with a circle of water.... The cross walks
> end in vistos, arches and statues, and the private ones cut
> thro' groves are delightful (Fig. 7). you think twenty times
> you have no more to see, and of a sudden find yourself in
> some new garden or walk, as finish'd and adorn'd as that
> you left. Nothing is more irregular in the whole, nothing
> more regular in the parts, which totally differ the one from
> the other. This shows my Lord's good tast, and his fondness
> to the place appears by the great expense he has been at.
> We all know how chargeable it is to make a garden with
> tast; to make one of a sudden is more so; but to erect so many
> Summer houses, Temples, Pillars, Piramids, and Statues,
> most of fine hewn stone, the rest of guilded lead, would drain
> the richest purse, and I doubt not but much of his wife's
> great fortune has been sunk in it. The Pyramid at the end of
> one of the walks is a copy in mignature of the most famous
> one in Egypt, and the only thing of the kind, I think, in
> England. Bridgman laid out the ground and plan'd the whole,
> which cannot fail of recommending him to business.[60]

---

[60] This letter was first published by A. Amherst in her *A History of Gardening in England*
(London, 1895); the letter is amongst the Egmont Papers, now B.M. Add. MSS 47030
fols. 156–9. I am indebted to Dr. P. Willis for this reference. Switzer already describes in
his 1715 edition a variety of garden structures: "I shall therefore add no more on this
Subject, when I have recommended the Erection of all Lodges, Granges, and other Buildings that Gentlemen are obliged to build, for Conveniency, in the Form of some Antiquated
Place, which will be more beautiful than the most curious Architecture: There seems to be

A sylvan seat existed in Cirencester Park, and Lord Bathurst invited Pope to come and sit upon it.[61] In 1721, it was replaced by King Alfred's Castle, a Gothic folly, and others were to follow.[62] At Chiswick, Burlington built only classical temples; at Claremont only the Belvedere is a medievalizing feature. Gibbs, of all people, had erected a Gothic temple at Stowe, and there is one by him in Shotover.[63] He also erected, according to his memoirs in Sir John Soane's Museum, "ornamental buildings" at Tring and similar buildings for Sir Thomas Lee near Aylesbury.[64] In his *Book of Architecture* of 1728 appear *tempietti*, urns, pavilions, obelisks, "shrines" (i.e. sheltered seats).[65] Two pavilions were planned for the grounds at Keddleston but were never built. Others might have been built; obviously there must have been considerable demand for such temples in the first quarter of the century long before the Landscape Garden existed.

The presence of these items of garden structures might derive from de Piles' or Lomazzo's descriptions, whether they all belong to one type, i.e. the heroic or the pastoral, that is classical or Gothic-inspired, or whether they appear mixed as de Piles would allow.[66] Their presence in gardens preceding the Landscape Garden is an indication that the associationism connected with them is a literary afterthought, but not their *raison d'être*. That must be looked for elsewhere.

The actual arrangement of garden structures at the end of a single vista or of a *patte d'oie*, as in Chiswick for instance, must derive from an actual prototype (Fig. 3). Chiswick bears a strong resemblance to the Teatro Olimpico in Vicenza with the important difference that at Chiswick Palladio's streets are garden paths. Burlington had recently returned from Vicenza, a convinced Palladian, and may have taken the opportunity to emulate the master.

----

a much more inexpressible Entertainment to a Virtuous and Thoughtful Mind, in Desolate Prospects, Cool murmuring Streams, and Grots, and in several other Cheap and Natural Embellishments, than in what many of our modern Designers have recommended, in themselves, very Expensive." (*Ichnographia*, here quoted from 2nd ed. [1718] I, 317).

[61] Hussey, *English Gardens*, 81.

[62] J. Lees-Milne, *Earls of Creation* (London, 1962), 54 and *passim*.

[63] L. Whistler, *Country Life*, 108 (1950), 1002; 122 (1957), 68.

[64] B. Little, *The Life and Work of James Gibbs* (London, 1955), 89.

[65] J. Gibbs, *Book on Architecture* (London, 1728), pls. LXVIII, LXX, LXXI, LXXII, LXXIX.

[66] See *supra*, pp. 16–17.

There are also stage designs with a similar arrangement of avenues (Fig. 8), one an Austrian one dating from the time of the Hapsburg emperor, Joseph I, designed by J. J. Sandrart (Fig. 9),[67] another in a design by Tacca for Cavalli's *L'Ipermestra* of 1658.[68] A similar design appears in 1745 in a tapestry by Charles de Vigne, obviously representing a (possibly much earlier) theatrical scene.[69]

A single vista with a terminal architectural feature is much more frequent. We can find it in French seventeenth century gardens, as Evelyn reports, and in Batty Langley's book on gardening of 1728 (Figs. 10, 11).[70] Langley suggests they be executed in canvas; Evelyn reports that this had occurred in the gardens he describes. Without doubt stage sets were painted on canvas. The single vista directed towards a terminal building is a most frequent feature on the stage— here, then, there is a direct relationship between garden and stage.

The close relationship between the vista in a garden, in a church or in a cortile is brought out in the caption of a design by Pozzo: "These *prospects* can be erected in the courtyard of a palace, in a garden, or could serve as a theatre for the forty hours devotion, as long as it could be viewed from a distance."[71] The view from a distance was important since these structures, too, were painted on canvas. Pozzo, in one case, makes fun of people who tried to climb up such a structure.[72]

Norbert Knopp, in his book on the Liechtenstein Belvedere in Vienna, pointed out that such a garden building, larger than the usual English garden temple, but less than a full-scale villa had the

[67] This design is reproduced in J. Gregor, *Denkmäler des Theaters: VII. Theater und Garten* (Munich, n.d. [1927]), pl. XIV.

[68] *L'Ipermestra*, Florence, 1658. Music by F. Cavalli, text by G. A. Moneghie, 12 engravings by Silvio degli Albi, after F. Tacca (1619–1686).

[69] H. Goebel, *Wandteppiche*, Part III, Vol. II (Berlin, 1934), pl. 62b. The date of this tapestry as well as its prototype is uncertain.

[70] J. Evelyn, *Diary* reported of such features in French and Italian gardens (cf. 27 February, 1644; 7 March, 1644; 1 April, 1644 and 2 April, 1644): "In the upper Walks are two Perspectives very pretty ones, seeming to enlarge the allys" (St. Cloud, 27 February, 1644); "... the Arch of Constantine in full size on a wall" (Richelieu Villa at Ruell, 27 February, 1644). B. Langley, *New Principles of Gardening* (London, 1728), xv.

[71] A. Pozzo, *Perspectiva pictorum et architectorum* (Rome, 1693), Part II, caption to fig. 48, "Questa inventione d'architettura potrebbe servire altresi per un Teatro di quarant'ore, ò per qualche altro luogo, onde potesse vedersi da lontano, come sarebbe nel fondo d'un giardino o pure nel cortile di un gran palazzo, non ho voluto tralasciar di metterlo in questo luogo per chi se ne volesse servire."

[72] *Ibid.*, caption to fig. 47.

same effect as such a building would have on the stage. Knopp goes on to analyze the Liechtenstein Belvedere and its position in the garden; he not only finds that it gives the feeling of a stage set, but also assumes that this arrangement derives genetically from a theatre setting.[73] There is at least one stage design reminiscent of Fischer's idea.[74]

A more direct link between garden and theatre exists when the garden is actually used as a theatre. Such examples are quite frequent on the Continent, for instance the Boboli Garden in Florence (Fig. 12) and the Zwinger in Dresden.[75] In Germany, temporary constructions were erected to serve as theatres and most eighteenth century gardens had a garden theatre. The perspective avenues were particularly suitable for theatrical purposes. There were a number of *Heckentheater* in Germany, as the one at Herrenhausen or at the Mirabell in Salzburg.[76] It seems from a painting of P. A. Rysbroek that such a theatre existed at Chiswick; in addition, there is the theatre *à la Serlio* at Claremont.

Although the link between theatre and garden seems possible, even probable, there is no proof that the designers and the patrons—those all-important men where gardens are concerned—connected de Piles' division of landscape painting with the Vitruvian and Serlian stage sets. Yet their knowledge of the texts and treatises may have led them to associate stage and garden design.

About the actual rise of the true Landscape Garden we are reasonably well informed. Despite Vanbrugh's saying, "you must get a Landskip Painter," which was first reported by Uvedale Price and is probably apocryphal,[77] one cannot doubt, indeed, that William Kent

---

[73] "Das Belvedere hat die Prospekthaftigkeit mit Bühnenbildern gemeinsam." N. Knopp *Das Garten-Belvedere* (Berlin, 1966), 79 and n. 159.

[74] A building rather like that by Fischer von Erlach for the Liechtenstein Belvedere occurs in a stage design by F. Guitti for *La Contesa*. A. Nicoll, *Stuart Masques and the Renaissance Stage* (London, 1937), 73, fig. 25.

[75] D. Coffin, *The Villa d'Este* (Princeton, 1960). Coffin quotes on the program of the villa: "in forma di Scena, ò Teatro semionta" (p. 25) and "Piazzetta ad uso di Teatro" (p. 177). Other examples are in the Villa Ludovisi, Villa Aldobrandini and Villa Torlonia, all in Frascati.

[76] R. Meyer, *Hecken- und Gartentheater in Deutschland im XVII und XVIII Jahrhundert* (Emsdetten, 1934). 131–138, 175–184; figs. 28–34, 56–58.

[77] Quoted by Hussey, *Picturesque*, 128. This is not the place to disprove Vanbrugh's status as landscape architect; it is just worth mentioning that Blenheim was landscaped by Brown, Wraywood of Castle Howard was a conventional wilderness (supra, n. 17) and the winding statue walk was the old village street. Letter of L. Whistler in *Country Life*, 95 (1944), 296.

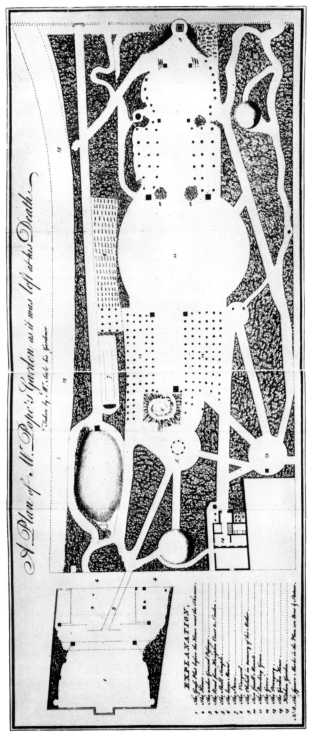

1. Plan of Pope's Garden by J. Serle, 1745, British Museum

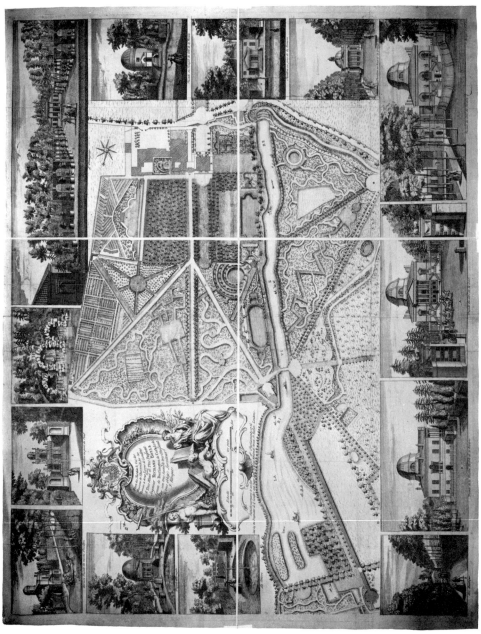

2. Plan of Chiswick House and Garden by J. Roque, 1736, British Museum

3. Chiswick House, *patte d'oie*, pen and ink drawing, Bodleian Library, Gough Coll., Oxford

4. Stowe, *View from Nelson's Seat*, by Chatelain, engr. by G. B. Bichham, 1753 (Oxford, Bodleian Library, Gough Coll.)

5. Stowe, plan of 1739, by S. Bridgeman

6. Stowe, plan of 1739, detail of fig. 5

7. Stowe, several garden buildings attributed to Vanbrugh, Gibbs, etc., engr. by G. L. Smith, after B. Seely (photo: N.M.R. Crown copyright)

8. Lodovico Burnacini, Design for *Il Pomo d'Oro*, Vienna, 1668, Victoria and Albert Museum E 116/1668 (photo: Crown copyright)

9. J. J. Sandrart, *Regia Virtutem...Regi Josepho I*, (photo:
from S. Gregor, *Denkmäler des Theaters, 7. Mappe, Theater
und Garten*, pl. 14)

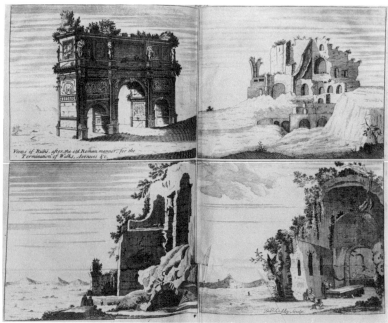

10. Batty Langley, "Ruins for the Termination of Avenues,"
New Principles of Gardening, 1728

11. Batty Langley, "An Avenue of Perspective," from *New Principles of Gardening*

12. Stefano della Bella, Scenes from a pageant held in Florence to celebrate the marriage of Cosimo III to Margherita Louise d'Orleans (Victoria and Albert Museum E 1583 1898, photo: Crown copyright)

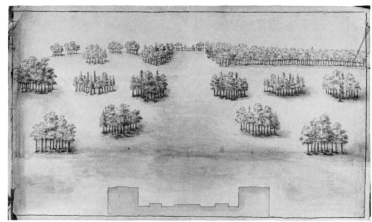

13. William Kent. Garden design, drawing (photo: Warburg Institute, by
permission of Lord Leicester of Holkham)

14. William Kent. Garden design, drawing (photo: Warburg Institute, by
permission of Lord Leicester of Holkham)

15. William Kent. Garden design, drawing (photo: Warburg Institute, by
permission of Lord Leicester of Holkham)

16. Inigo Jones, design for a Masque, Devonshire Collection, Chatsworth
(Reproduced by permission of the Trustees of the Chatsworth Settlement)

17. Stowe, Temple of Ancient Virtue (photo: N.M.R. Crown Copyright)

18. Filippo Juvarra. Stage design for *Tempio di Diana per l'Ifigenia in Tauri*, Turin, Bibl. Naz. Ris. 59, ra, 85(1)
(photo: from M. Viale Ferrero, *Filippo Juvarra*)

19. Stourhead. View of lake and gardens (photo: N.M.R. Crown copyright)

20. Stourhead. View of Pantheon and setting (photo: N.M.R. Crown copyright)

21. S. Switzer, "A Forest or Rural Garden," *Ichnographia*, 1718, III, 44

created the Landscape Garden, as Walpole reports.[78] There is a contemporary document that mentions Kent and gives a fairly definite date. In 1734, Sir Thomas Robinson wrote to his father-in-law Lord Carlisle as follows:

> There is a new taste in gardening just arisen which has been practiced with so great success at the Prince's garden in Town [i.e., at Richmond] that a general alteration of some of the most considerable gardens in the Kingdom is begun, after Mr. Kent's notion, viz. to lay them out and work without level or line. By this means I really think the twelve acres the Prince's garden consists of, is more diversified and of greater variety than anything of that compass I ever saw, and this method of gardening is the more agreeable as, when finished, it has the appearance of beautiful nature, and without being told, one would imagine art had no part in the finishing, and is, according to what one knows of the Chinese, entirely after their models for works of this nature where they never plant straight lines or make regular designs. The celebrated gardens of Claremont, Chiswick and Stowe are now full of labourers to modernise the expensive works finished in them even since everyone's memory. If this grows a fashion, 'twill be happy for that class of people, as they will run no risk of having time lay on their hands.[79]

This is a curious document: it is an historical document, but at the same time an echo of the literary tradition of the description as a form of rhetorical exercise. The letter also indicates that the Landscape Garden movement, at that moment anyhow, was still somewhat esoteric and restricted to the narrow circle of the Palladians round Burlington.

The Burlington circle was able to draw on yet another source, almost certainly available only to them. Father Matteo Ripa had brought an album of engravings of Chinese gardens to the West. It came into the

[78] H. Walpole, *The History of the Modern Taste in Gardening*, ed. I. W. V. Chase (Princeton, 1943), 25 and *passim*. Spence, *Anecdotes*, I, 251 § 603, quotes Southcote as saying "Mr. Pope and Kent were the first that practised painting in gardening ... [but] Kent had little more than the idea of mixing lighter and darker greens ..."

[79] Quoted by Hussey, *English Gardens*, 45, without reference; the letter is presumably at Castle Howard.

hands of Lord Burlington and is now in the British Museum. It has recently been discussed by Wittkower who made out a case for its great influence, particularly on the Whigs. He thought the engravings instrumental in bringing about the Landscape Garden.[80] Burlington and his circle certainly recognized in the engravings the prototype of Temple's Sharawadgi. Yet, had they set out to emulate these Chinese gardens, would they not have added Chinese temples to their garden architecture? But there are none at that time in England; later a Chinese house appeared at Shugborough in 1747,[81] and Chambers put his pagoda into Kew.[82]

The engravings must have created a stir, and they confirmed Temple's and Addison's views on *Sharawadgi*. Against a direct transference of these Chinese prototypes the same objections can be raised as against that of Claude's or Gaspard's pictures, namely the psychological difficulty of transforming a two-dimensional image into three-dimensional reality. It could be said of course that a stage design was no different from any other "two-dimensional" drawing; yet there is one vital difference: a stage design intended for execution must be translatable into three-dimensional reality in such a way that the spectator in the theatre believes he has an actual town- or landscape in front of him. True, there will be a large backdrop, but also wings and architectural structures real or fictitious, which must all be so arranged that they seem real, their distances and foreshortening correct from a perspectival point of view. All that is probably not so in landscape of Claude or Salvator Rosa. Perhaps one might add that in many literary quotations and in descriptions of gardens "perspective" was much stressed and often in actual gardens including landscape gardens the vista much in evidence, not only along avenues, but also in glades, even across fields; structures were erected to make an "object" from the house, as e.g. a Gothic ruin in Rousham.

Kent was not the first to leap the fence; the ha-ha had been used, albeit in a limited way, by Bridgeman, and its predecessor was men-

[80] R. Wittkower, "English Neo-Palladianism," 18–35.

[81] In J. Harris, *Sir William Chambers, Knight of the Star*, with contributions by J. M. Crook and E. Harris (London, 1970), 147. E. Harris enumerates the following Chinese garden buildings: a Chinese hut at Stowe (1746), a summerhouse at Shugborough (1748), a lodge and summerhouse at Wroxton, a Temple of Confucius designed by Chambers for Frederick, Prince of Wales.

[82] Pagoda, 1761–62. Harris, *op. cit.*, 213 (50).

tioned by Alberti, though disapprovingly, as having been recommended by one Democritus: "And indeed what we are told *Democritus* very much condemned, namely, the inclosing a Garden with any Sort of Wall, I should not blame in the Case before us, but am rather of Opinion, that it is a very proper Defense against Malice or Rapine."[83]

Nor can one truthfully say that the Landscape Garden, looks like the English landscape.[84] To the beholder of the English countryside any present or former landscape garden stands out quite clearly. The type of trees, their arrangement and the general planting within the garden are strikingly different from the countryside without.

Some of the features of Kent's garden derive unquestionably from Italian gardens: the cascade at Rousham closely resembles one at the gardens of the Villa Barberigo at Valzansibio near Padua, and the exedra at Chiswick is similar to a feature in the gardens of Duke Mattei on Monte Celio in Rome.[85] Generally speaking, Italian gardens of the seventeenth century were more leafy than the contemporary English gardens, the trees feathery and parts of the gardens were always "irregular", "wild" and "natural." England had borrowed so much from Italy, why not their gardens?[86]

Was the decisive factor again, as in the earlier phases of the eighteenth century garden, the influence of the theatre? (Figs. 13, 14, 15) Kent who had started his artistic career as a painter, later in life made stage sets on at least two occasions.[87] Thus, he would have been the right man to strengthen the link.[88] There are at least two examples of a similarity between a stage set and a garden design by Kent too close to be accidental: one, a design for a court masque from the circle

---

[83] *De Re Aedificatoria*, IX, iv.

[84] B. S. Allen, *Tides in English Taste (1619–1800)* (Cambridge, 1937, reprinted New York, 1958), ch. 18, "The Artifice of the Natural Garden," (II, 149–159).

[85] Illustrated in G. B. Falda, *Li Giardini di Roma* (Rome, n.d.), pl. 17.

[86] See also most recently, MacDougall, "*Ars Hortulorum*,", and n. 35 *supra*.

[87] Kent designed the scenery for Nicolo Porpora's *La Festa d'Imeneo*, 1736. See E. Croft Murray, Review of M. Jourdain, *William Kent* (London, 1949), *Country Life*, 105 (1949), 269; and for John Gay's *The Captives*, idem, *Decorative Painting in England: 1537–1837*, II (London, 1970), 231.

[88] There is one other design, which is usually interpreted as a design for Pope's Shell Temple, although M. Mack has thrown doubts on this attribution. It certainly belonged to Pope and used to be attributed to him, since the original in the British Museum (1872-11-9-878) is endorsed to the son of Pope's housekeeper. But for two people, one holding a palette, the other binoculars, and a dog, one could take this drawing, with a group of nymphs and a rainbow and a sacrifice inside the temple, for a stage design.

round Inigo Jones, is echoed at Stowe (Figs. 16, 17);[89] the other, a stage set by Juvarra (Figs. 18, 19, 20), resembles a corner at Stourhead. Mercedes Viale Ferrero, the author of a recent book on Juvarra's stage designs, remarking on this likeness, has actually suggested that Kent might have been present at a performance in Rome of the play and have seen the set.[90]

Designs by both Inigo Jones and Juvarra were available to Kent through Lord Burlington. Burlington acquired the large collection of Jones's designs that now forms the Burlington Devonshire Collection at Chatsworth, and Kent acted as an editor of a volume of Inigo Jones's architectural designs, adding a few of his own.[91] Inigo Jones designed many landscape settings for masques and also, in one design, imitated very closely Serlio's illustration of the satyric scene.[92]

The country of stage design had been Italy. Italian stage designs from the early eighteenth century could have reached England through three channels: engravings of the oeuvre of Italian stage designers, illustrated textbooks, and in addition an actual link between Burlington and Juvarra.

Juvarra also designed many landscape settings; they were even more free and asymmetrical than those of Inigo Jones.[93] It is possible

[89] Now at Chatsworth. The design was for *The Triumph of the Prince d'Amour*, scene 5.

[90] M. Viale Ferrero, *Filippo Juvarra, scenografo e architetto teatrale* (Turin, 1970), 56, "Tempio di Diana per l'Ifigenia in Tauri." (Turin, Bibl. Naz. Ris. 59, 4a 85(1)). The temple at Stourhead was only put up in 1754, six years after Kent's death, but may, of course, have been designed earlier. K. Woodbridge, *Landscape and Antiquity* (Oxford, 1970), 33, 35, suggests tentatively—although admitting that the link of Claude's *Aneas at Delos* with the Pantheon at Stourhead must remain conjectural—that the path round the lake was an allegory of Aneas's journey adding that there is an inscription in the Temple of Flora from the Sixth Book, "Procul, o procul este profani." G. B. Clark "The History of Stowe. XIII, Kent and the Eastern Gardens," *Stoic*, 24, (1971) 265–271, esp. 268 ff. also suggests an iconographical interpretation for Stowe. See now, idem, "Grecian Taste and Gothic Virtue: Lord Cobham's Gardening Programme and its Iconography," *Apollo* 97 (1973), 566–571.

[91] Published in 1727 (*W. Kent, The Designs of Inigo Jones*, London, 1727). These drawings now forming the Burlington-Devonshire Collection were acquired by Burlington in 1723. *Catalogue of the R.I.B.A., Sir Banister Fletcher Library Collection*, I (London, 1960), 84.

[92] These designs are now in the Burlington-Devonshire Collection at Chatsworth and have been partially published and discussed, first by P. Simpson and C. F. Bell, "Designs by Inigo Jones for Masques and Plays at Court," *Walpole Society*, 12 (1924). There is also a recent exhibition cataloque, *Festival Designs by Inigo Jones*, Intro. and Cat. by R. Strong (n.p., 1967). In addition, reproductions have appeared in many books on masques.

[93] Viale Ferrero, *Juvarra*, e.g., figs. 76, 140, 141, 145, 149, 164; (the Temple, 146). For a discussion of landscape on the stage see E. Gronewald, *Garten und Landschaftsgestaltung auf der Bühne im 16. und 17. Jahrhundert* (Berlin, 1940). For a discussion of the landscape stage sets of Inigo Jones see H. Richter, *Harms J. O.* (Emsdetten, 1963), 175, 178. Cf. H. Tintelnot, *Barocktheater und barocke Kunst* (Berlin, 1939), 38.

that Kent might have seen Juvarra sets at stage performances in Rome. In addition, Juvarra was in England in 1720 and on that occasion was in close contact with Burlington. Further evidence of the link is provided by a sketchbook of architectural phantasies dedicated to Lord Burlington and dated 1730.[94] Could it be that Kent, when on a visit to Rome in that year, acted as a messenger? In addition, editions of plays with illustrations of Juvarra's sets may have been available in England.

As stage designer, Kent would have been able to visualise and to carry out a three-dimensional design of some complexity and to fit the temples and ruins into it (Figs. 13, 14, 15).[95] Often such garden structures were included in stage sets. Must we then believe that an accident of history produced, at a moment when there was an outcry for a natural garden and stage designs became available that could be used as models, the right men who could invent and carry out this new idea?

Summarizing, one can say that there was a literary genre which might have been influential, but did not actually bring about the landscape garden. Again at some later moment, Claude and Gaspard might have contributed, but the true progenitor of the landscape garden of its first and second phase was stage design and its written emanations, evolving from Vitruvius and particularly from the Renaissance tradition.

[94] R. Wittkower, "Un libro di schizzi di Filippo Juvarra a Chatsworth," *Bollettino della Società Piemontese d' archaeologia e di belle arti*, 3 (1949), 1–25.

[95] Kent owned Pietro Accolti's *Prosepettiva Practica* in *Libri di Prospettiva*, ed. G. Troili (Bologna, 1683); he copied several perspective drawings in his diary (Bodley MS. Rawlinson D 1162, ff. 13r, 26v, 27r, 27v), amongst them one for a stage construction (f. 27r). Although he there acknowledges it to Accolti, the design derives from an illustration in G. Troili, *Per Praticare la Prospettiva senza saperla* (Bologna, 1683), xlviii.

Eighteenth Century Amateur Architects and their Gardens

Michael McCarthy

"So many men of taste of all ranks devoted themselves to the new improvements," Horace Walpole wrote in 1770, "that it is surprising how much beauty has been struck out, with how few absurdities." He referred here to improvements in the style of landscape gardening, which he charted as a progressive development, from closed to open form, from straight to sinuous line, from the practice of London and Wise to that of William Kent and Lancelot Brown.[1]

The particular purpose of this paper is to bring to light the extent of the contribution of those men of taste, the amateur architects of the third quarter of the eighteenth century, to the practice of landscape gardening in England. The subject cannot be defined solely in terms of the physical changes to their estates effected by amateur architects by way of the movement of earth and the plantation of trees. Little evidence of that type of change remains, for family papers will normally record only undifferentiated payments of lump sums to the gardener, or on the gardening account. Only where a professional designer was called in to advize can we hope for a separate payment of greater specificity, and in such cases the estates obviously do not qualify for inclusion in this paper. What evidence we have can be adequately treated within the context of a discussion of the garden buildings designed by amateur architects, and this approach should prove rewarding. For, as Sir John Summerson has pointed out, the design of garden buildings is related in a fundamental way to the

---

[1] H. Walpole, *Anecdotes of Painting in England*, ed. R. Wornum, III (London, 1888), 85.

changes in concepts of garden design, and Robert Adam's declaration of the importance of "movement" in architecture can be seen as the culmination of a trend apparent at least as early as Burlingtonian designs for garden buildings.[2] The intimate relationship between architecture and gardening in the eighteenth century was succinctly expressed by Thomas Whately in 1770, in the opening pages of his *Observations on Modern Gardening:* "Nature, always simple, employs but four materials in the composition of her scenes, *ground, wood, water,* and *rocks.* The cultivation of nature has introduced a fifth species, the *buildings* requisite for the accommodation of men."[3]

Richard Grenville, Lord Temple, who owned Stowe House and its gardens in Buckinghamshire, was the most important of the amateur architects of the period who took an active part in the designing of landscape gardens. His contribution to the art has not, however, been recognized, for the histories of gardening and architecture alike tend to ignore the works of amateurs and patrons in favour of those of professional architects and landscape-designers. Yet the subject is important, because if Stowe gardens owe much to Lord Temple, the whole history of gardening owes much to him. The bibliography of Stowe in the eighteenth century is sufficient indication of its importance to contemporaries,[4] and Christopher Hussey has pointed to Stowe as the most important source of the *jardin anglais* for continental landscape architects.[5]

Stowe gardens, of course, had a long and very honourable history before Richard Grenville assumed control of them in 1749. This history has recently been clarified by George Clarke, who for the first time has taken into consideration the evidence on the subject afforded by the papers relating to Stowe which are in the Henry E. Huntington Library. For our purposes, it is important to note that his examination of this evidence has led him to the conclusion that Richard Temple, Lord Cobham, who then owned Stowe, was as important a figure in the creation and development of Stowe gardens as either

---

[2] J. Summerson, *Architecture in Britain, 1530–1830* (London, 1969), 203, 288.

[3] T. Whately, *Observations on Modern Gardening* (Dublin, 1770), 2.

[4] The most complete bibliography is to be found in L. Whistler, M. Gibbon and G. Clarke, *Stowe: A Guide to the Gardens* (Buckingham, 1968), 37–38.

[5] C. Hussey, *English Gardens and Landscapes, 1700–1750* (London, 1967), 89. See also L. M. Wiggin, *The Faction of Cousins* (New Haven, 1958), 55–58.

William Kent or Lancelot Brown.[6] Further research among the Stowe Papers has revealed that Lord Cobham's nephew and successor, Richard Grenville, who became Lord Temple in 1752, was a worthy successor in that he personally planned and supervized the growth and expansion of Stowe gardens, which, to quote a contemporary author, were "esteemed by persons of the most exact taste to be the finest in this kingdom, and perhaps in Europe."[7]

Indeed, the Stowe Papers leave no doubt of the personal involvement of the future Lord Temple in the shaping of Stowe gardens long before the death of Lord Cobham. His account book records payments to Lancelot Brown in 1742, 1744 and 1746, and he paid one Williamson the sizeable sum of £6.10.6 for trees for Stowe in 1744.[8]

Ironically, the principal document that substantiates the claim that Lord Temple was a landscape designer refers not to Stowe, but to Eastbury in Dorsetshire, a Vanbrugh-Bridgeman work as Stowe had been. Built from about 1715, Eastbury came into the possession of Lord Temple by inheritance in 1762.[9] The original plan for the gardens by Bridgeman survives, and it shows us no surprises. The lord of Stowe, who had distinguished his estate by keeping it always in the forefront of changes in landscape design, could not be expected to be sympathetic to a plan that was characteristic of the previous generation of designers. We learn from a letter of his younger brother, Henry Grenville, who lived at Eastbury, that Lord Temple redesigned the gardens of Eastbury:

> The new improvements at Eastbury, in the alteration of the water etc., as planned and projected by your Lordship, already begin to make a figure. The work goes on briskly, and so it ought, for a handsome number of hands are employ-

[6] G. Clarke, "Lancelot Brown's Work at Stowe," *The Stoic*, December 1971, 21–22. Clarke's account of the earlier gardens at Stowe is to be found in the following numbers of *The Stoic*: March 1968; December 1969; March 1970; July 1970; July 1971. See now *idem*, "The Gardens of Stowe," "Grecian Taste and Gothic Virtue: Lord Cobham's Gardening Programme and Its Iconography," *Apollo*, 97 (1973), 558–565, 566–571.

[7] Quoted from B. S. Allen, *Tides in English Taste*, II (New York, 1969), 140.

[8] Richard, Earl Temple's Personal Account Book, 1732–1779, fols. 125, 144, 146, 158, in manuscript among the Stowe Papers.

[9] For Eastbury house see L. Whistler, *The Imagination of Vanbrugh and his Fellow-Artists* (London, 1954), 156–77. For Eastbury gardens see P. Willis, "Charles Bridgeman: Royal Gardener," Ph. D. diss., Cambridge University, n.d. In a letter dated August 17, 1763, among the Stowe Papers, (Box 107), Lord Temple complained to Thomas Wyndham that the building accounts of Eastbury had disappeared, and that the chapel was still unfinished.

ed. Old Upjohn, our first operator for the pond, has been tried and found but one degree better than an old woman. His science, besides, went no further than making it with one stratum of clay, then one of chalk, and so on. He therefore has been dismissed, and another found in his room, a pondmaker *dans toutes les règles*, strongly recommended as fit for the business, and who deals in chalk only, and with chalk only will undertake and perfect the mighty work. This circumstance weighs strongly in Harvey's mind and in mine, as it will be a great saving of labour and expence. And yet with all our savings, ploughing and carting with my own horses, so he cannot bring himself to think that the whole of the work will cost less than £200—he even has his doubts if so little. I am now plunged so deep in carts and wheelbarrows, and all the implements of garden work, that I scare know when I shall get free; but pardon me, my dear Brother, this one work of extravagance (I cannot quite find it in my heart to call it folly). This one work once accomplished, I certainly shall not seek to engage you, or myself, in another.[10]

There is, alas, little else to tell of Eastbury. Lord Temple did not proceed with the alterations he had designed for the gardens there, as we learn from a letter of the same correspondent written to the Stowe steward, Joseph Parrott, five years later:

I much regret the forlorn state of Eastbury. Whilst I lived there everything flourished and seemed to smile, tho' not without great pains, constant attention, and as constant an expence to me. My living there was a great and substantial prop, not only to the beauty, but even to the preservation of the place itself. That prop, alas, is now withdrawn, and whatever support it receives now must be derived from Lord Temple himself. If he thinks proper to keep it up, the credit as well as the expence will be his own; if he suffers a place so magnificent in itself to sink into a state of desolation and

[10] Stowe Papers, Box 10, marked also L 7.A 5. This letter is dated from Eastbury, October 21, 1767.

decay, the fault will not be mine—I did a great deal for its sake, but I hear it is terribly neglected now.[11]

This letter was written in 1772, and one can assume that Lord Temple did not invest further time and money in maintaining East-bury gardens, since the main block of the mansion house was blown up on his orders three years later.[12]

However, Lord Temple was devoting most of his time and money to the improvement of the Stowe estate in those years. He was un-doubtedly the architect of the landscaping there after the death of Lord Cobham in 1749, an event that coincided with the departure of Lancelot Brown from the gardens of Stowe, and with the appointment of Richard Woodward as his successor. Woodward's background is not known; but there is no indication in the Stowe Papers, or elsewhere, that he was reponsible for designing alterations to landscape gardens. However, we find several positive indications of Lord Temple's active involvement in the architectural changes that took place at Stowe in these years, and there is at least one reference which demonstrates his control of changes in the landscape garden. In a letter of 11 Febru-ary 1772 to his steward, he wrote: "I cannot fix anything concerning Wotton avenue but on the spot, so you may take elsewhere what may be wanted; Regard being had not to disfigure."[13]

From another source comes evidence of the fame of Lord Temple as a designer of improvements twenty years earlier. Robert Nugent, later Lord Clare, wrote from Gosfield Hall, Essex, to Sanderson Miller, then visiting Stowe, and added to the letter a postscript addressed to Lord Temple, which ends with the exhortation: "Come here and bring Mr. Pitt with you. Give me plans, persuade me to execute them."[14] It is unlikely that the plans mentioned were for buildings,

[11] Stowe Papers, Box marked Stowe Business 234a, letter dated from Geneva, February 22, 1772.

[12] A letter from William Doggett to Lord Temple, dated from Eastbury, June 29, 1774, which is in the Stowe Papers, Box 110, shows that Lord Temple was spending money on the repair of the house up to that time. One Hiscock was the mason in charge. There can be little basis in fact for the story that Lord Temple offered two hundred pounds annually to anyone who would live in Eastbury house; his younger brother was clearly very happy to live there until failing health forced him to convalesce on the continent.

[13] Stowe Papers, Box 107.

[14] L. Dickins and M. Stanton, *An Eighteenth-Century Correspondence* (London, 1910), 238–9. The fullest account of William Pitt's landscape gardening is still B. Williams, *Life of William Pitt*, I (London, 1915), 190–202. Further details are given below, pp. 49–50.

because Sanderson Miller had already been entrusted with designing the new wing for Gosfield Hall.[15] Besides, Lord Temple's brother-in-law, William Pitt, enjoyed a high reputation as a landscape-designer, and the mention of his name with that of Lord Temple leads us to believe that landscaping was in question rather than buildings.[16]

It should not be inferred from this, however, that Lord Temple did not design garden buildings as well as gardens. There are many indications to the contrary, the most visual one, even if it is not the most persuasive, being his portrait of 1760 in the National Portrait Gallery, London, by William Hoare. (Fig. 1). This shows him seated at a table, with his hand resting on a plan of the Temple of Concord and Victory at Stowe. This pose is so often met with in the portraits of amateur architects of the period that it might almost be considered a portrait convention. Witness William Hogarth's portrait of Theodore Jacobsen at Oberlin, in which the sitter holds a print of the elevation and plan of the Foundling Hospital, which he had designed. There is a comparable portrait of John Eld in the Boston Museum of Fine Arts, by Gainsborough. Similar portraits exist of Sir Roger Newdigate by Arthur Devis at Arbury Hall, of Lord Fauconburgh at Newburgh Priory, of Thomas Prowse at Berkeley House. The portrait of John Chute by Gabriel Matthias at The Vyne in Hampshire shows the sitter holding the Gothic elevation which he proposed for the south front of that house in 1769.[17] In all these cases we know the subject of the portrait to have been the designer of the building shown, so it is at least probable that Lord Temple's pose in the Hoare portrait constitutes a claim to have been the designer of that remarkable building.[18]

A recent study by Michael Gibbon of the Temple of Concord and Victory, first called the Grecian Temple (Fig. 2), and earlier studies by Laurence Whistler and Christopher Hussey, have pointed to its

---

[15] A. C. Woods and W. Hawkes, "Sanderson Miller of Radway and His Work at Wroxton," *Cake and Cockhorse*, Banbury Historical Society, 4 (1969), no. 6, 108.

[16] For an account of Gosfield see C. Nugent, *Memoirs of Earl Nugent* (London, 1898), 10–12.

[17] The date is given by an inscription of Horace Walpole on a drawing of the proposed south front of The Vyne by John Chute, in the Lewis Walpole Library, Farmington, Connecticut, (Chute Album, 28). It is quoted here by kind permission of Wilmarth S. Lewis.

[18] This cannot be regarded as conclusive evidence, however. Michael Dahl's portrait of Henry Hoare I, at Stourhead, shows him holding the elevation of that house, which was designed by Colin Campbell. See K. Woodbridge, *Landscape and Antiquity* (London, 1970), 18–20 and plate 21b.

importance, and that of the Grecian Valley which it dominated, as the first indication of the archaeological approach to design which is associated with neo-classicism.[19] The creation of the valley was one of the most ambitious of the alterations at Stowe, and much excavation was required to hollow out the L-shaped area, which, lying to the north-east of the house directly above the Elysian Fields, bent eastward at the site of the temple to close the area north of Hawkewell Field.[20]

Everything in Stowe's gardens took on a larger scale under the direction of Lord Temple. The plantations were softened and broadened and serpentined to a degree that can be appreciated only by comparing a map of the gardens as they were in 1753, (Fig. 3), four years after he succeeded to the estate, with a map made in 1777 (Fig. 4), two years before his death. It became incumbent upon the garden buildings, if they were to hold their place in this more open landscape, to take on a comparable scale. This is what happened. The garden buildings erected at Stowe between 1749 and 1779, namely the Temple of Concord and Victory, the Corinthian Arch, and the Ladies' Buildings, were built on a scale unprecedented at Stowe or elsewhere. Only the Doric Arch is on the scale of the pre-1749 garden buildings, and this is probably because its purpose was to admit visitors to the earlier and more intimate Elysian Fields, which had been designed by William Kent. The alterations effected by Lord Temple to older buildings, particularly to Vanbrugh's Rotunda and Gibbs's Boycott Pavilions, were equally telling in this respect. These have been adequately documented by earlier writers on Stowe, and Hussey has happily characterised the effect of these alterations in writing that they induce a "sostenuto" rhythm in harmony with the softer and more open landscape, rather than a "staccato" rhythm created by buildings which functioned visually as terminal points in more rigidly designed gardens.[21] My concern will be with the later buildings, those which I mentioned above as built newly under Lord Temple's direction. Recent research among the Stowe Papers allows me to

[19] M. Gibbon, "Lord Cobham's Garden Buildings, Part 2," *The Stoic*, December 1970, 208–15; L. Whistler, "The Authorship of the Stowe Temples," *Country Life*, 108 (1950), 1002–6; Hussey, *English Gardens*, 109–110.

[20] Clarke, "Brown at Stowe," summarizes the information available from the Stowe Papers relating to the excavation of the Grecian Valley.

[21] Hussey, *English Gardens*, 106.

throw some light upon their authorship and dates of building, and thereby prompts some reflections upon the relationship of garden design to the design of garden buildings in the second half of the eighteenth century.

In the Stowe Papers, the Grecian Valley is first mentioned as the Grecian Diagonal on 9 May 1747. Since this date coincides with the completion of Lord Cobham's Pillar at the eastern end of the valley, there is some reason to suppose that the provision of a rewarding view from the top of that pillar, to north as well as to the south, precipitated the decision to take the area north-east of the house into the gardening scheme, which had hitherto been confined to the south.[22] Not until 1749, however, the year of Lord Cobham's death and Lord Temple's succession, did work begin on the construction of the Grecian Temple, at the point of the bend in the valley. Its construction was was not rapid, and the details were still being decided by Lord Temple in collaboration with the architect Giovanni Battista Borra in 1752, when the latter wrote from London on July 3:

> I received your note with the drawing of the Temple, and I am very happy to learn that the wood of the roof will rise higher than is indicated in the section of the drawing, for this makes it possible to have a more complete cornice about the Peristyle. I have the honour of sending you this: and should you wish that it be ornamented, please send it back to me, so that I can mark the places where the ornaments should go.[23]

The implication of this letter is clearly that someone other than Borra had designed the fabric of the building. It has traditionally been attributed to William Kent, but the earliest date of that attribution is 1788, exactly forty years after Kent's death, and Gibbon has recently shown convincing reasons for doubting this attribution. The portrait by William Hoare indicates that Lord Temple was the architect, and it is now clear that Borra's role was to design the ornamental details.

---

[22] Between November 22, 1746 and September 29, 1747, Richard Batchelor was paid a total of £82.14.10½ for building the pillar known as the Cobham Monument. The bills are among the Stowe Papers, Box marked Stowe Building and Repair Accounts 1710–47. The pillar was later altered to designs by Valdré; see Gibbon, *Cobham's Buildings*, 207.

[23] Stowe Papers, Box marked Stowe Business 108. Eight letters from G. B. Borra to Lord Temple survive, three of 1752, five of 1754. All are addressed from London.

1. William Hoare, *Portrait of Richard Grenville, Lord Temple*, 1760, National Portrait Gallery, London

2. The Temple of Concord and Victory, Stowe, 1749–63, here attributed to Lord Temple
(photo: courtesy of *Country Life*)

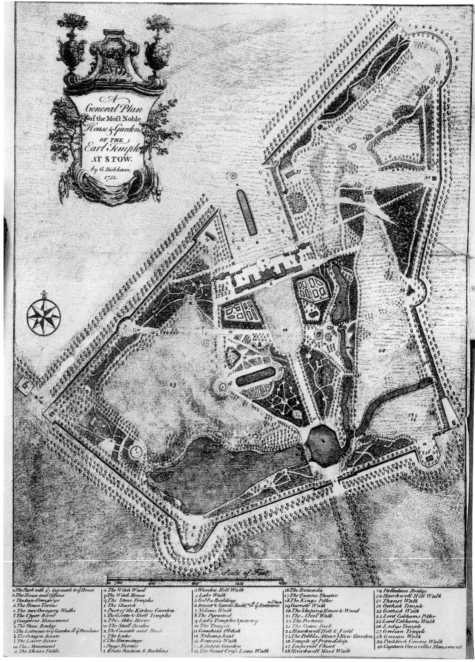

3. Plan of Stowe Gardens, 1753, by G. Bickham (photo: courtesy of the Courtauld Institute of Art, London, and of Stowe School)

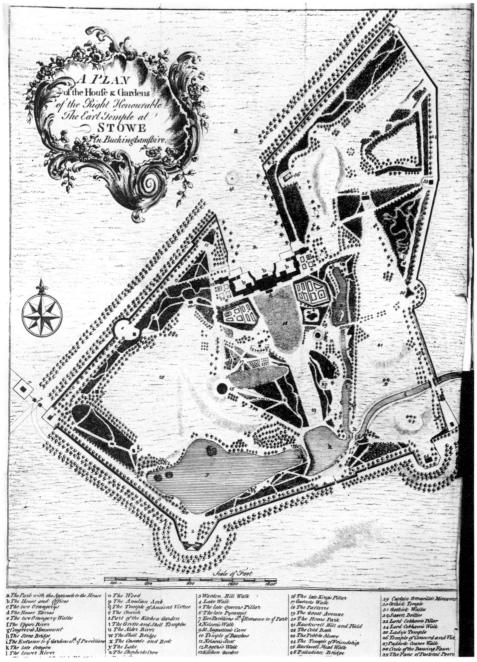

4. Plan of Stowe Gardens, 1777, by B. Seeley (photo: courtesy of the Courtauld Institute of Art, London, and of Stowe School)

5. Ornamentation of the Temple of Concord and Victory, Stowe, 1752–63, here attributed to Lord Temple and G. B. Borra (photo: courtesy of *Country Life*)

6. The Corinthian Arch, Stowe, 1765–7, by Thomas Pitt

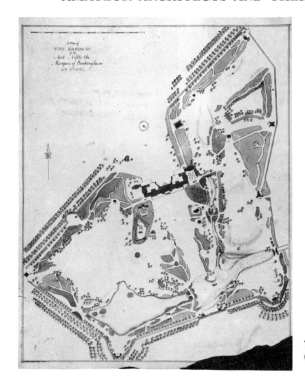

7. Plan of Stowe Gardens, 1797, by anonymous artist
(photo: courtesy of the Courtauld Institute of Art, London,
and of Stowe School)

8. Sir Joshua Reynolds, *Portrait of Thomas Pitt, Lord
Camelford*, Boconnoc House, Cornwall, England (photo:
Robert Chapman, Plymouth, England)

9. Plan of Stowe Gardens, 1753, by G. Bickham, detail of fig. 3

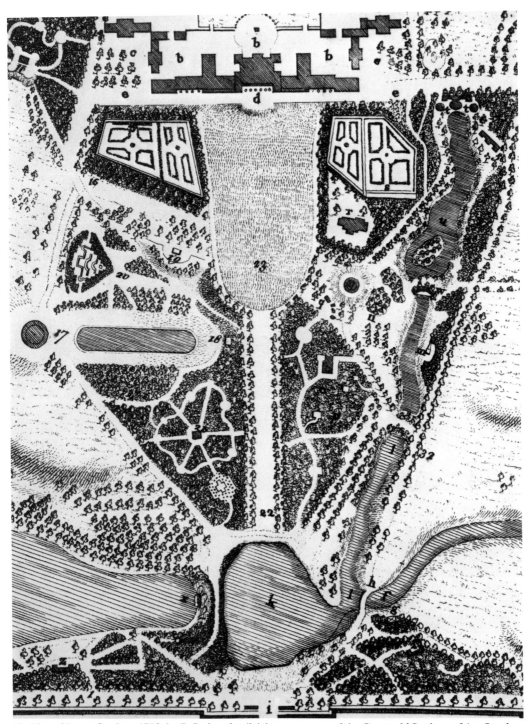

10. Plan of Stowe Gardens, 1756, by B. Seeley, detail (photo: courtesy of the Courtauld Institute of Art, London, and of Stowe School)

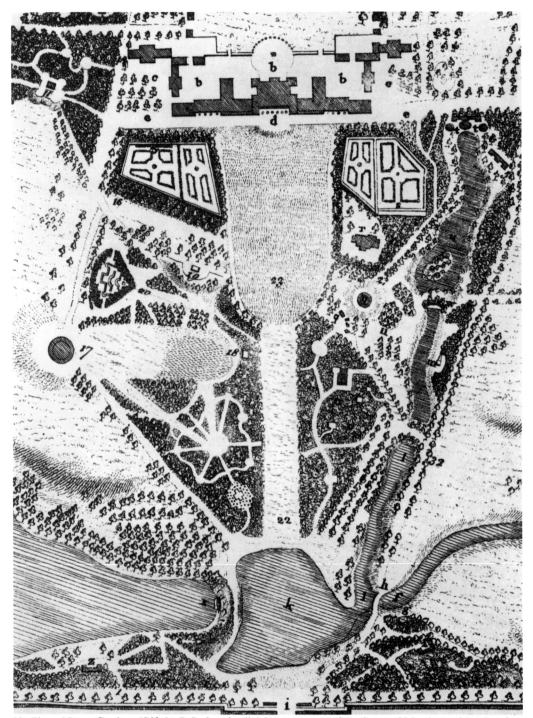

11. Plan of Stowe Gardens, 1763, by B. Seeley, detail (photo: courtesy of the Courtauld Institute of Art, London, and of Stowe School)

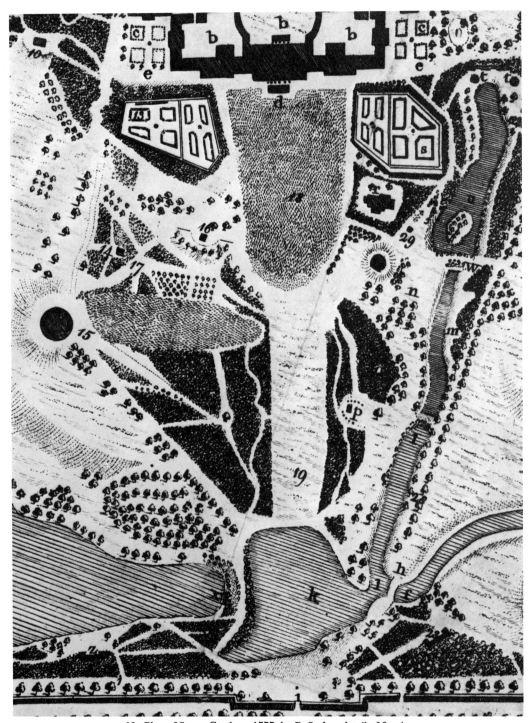

12. Plan of Stowe Gardens, 1777, by B. Seeley, detail of fig. 4

13. The Doric Arch, Stowe, 1768, here
attributed to Lord Temple (photo: courtesy
of Stowe School)

14. The Ladies' Temple, Stowe, South front, 1772–7,
here attributed to Thomas Pitt (photo: courtesy of
Stowe School)

15. The Ladies' Temple, Stowe, north front, 1772–7,
here attributed to Thomas Pitt (photo: courtesy of
Country Life)

16. Anonymous, *A View in Hagley Park* (photo: courtesy of Kenneth Woodbridge)

17. William Hoare, *Portrait of William Pitt*, c. 1754, National
Portrait Gallery, London

18. Rev. T. Streatfeild, *A View in Hagley Park*, c. 1820 (photo: courtesy of Sabin Galleries, London)

19. Detail of fig. 18, showing the Palladian bridge by Thomas Pitt, c. 1763

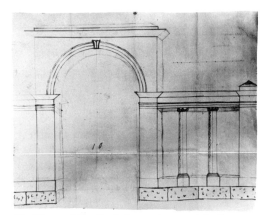

20. Thomas Pitt, *Sketch for an entrance arch for Boconnoc* c. 1780, Sir John Soane's Museum, London

J. B. Chatelain's drawing of the temple, engraved by George Bickham in 1753, shows it completed structurally, but without its sculptures. However, Borra's next letter to Lord Temple, dated 9 July 1752, shows that he designed the statues in that year: "As for the drawing of the statue of Flora, I have not put in any scale, so that you may make it as big as you wish. However, I think that the statue of Hero should be lifesize."[24]

It was some time, however, before the ornamentation of the temple (Fig. 5) was completed. We know that the sculptor James Lovell carved flowers and other ornaments for the plasterers from 1752 to 1754.[25] We also know that the windows and the door were ready to be sent from London for setting up in 1755.[26] However, the sculptor William Stephenson, who had carved a bas-relief for the pediment of Liverpool Town Hall in 1752,[27] did not start work on the pediment of the Grecian Temple at Stowe until 1761, when he adapted Peter Scheemakers's relief sculpture, *Britannia Receiving Homage*, to squeeze it rather awkwardly into its present location. He worked for ten weeks at a weekly salary of one pound ten shillings, and had travelling expenses of ten shillings weekly.[28] The building was considered complete by 1763, the date carved on the pediment. In that year it was re-named the Temple of Concord and Victory, to commemmorate the successful conclusion of the Seven Years' War under the prime-ministership of Lord Temple's brother-in-law and colleague in landscape gardening, William Pitt. Five years later the inscriptions in the interior were added in consultation with Lord Lyttelton of Hagley, to whom Lord Temple wrote: "I have found some fine words, I think, for the frieze of the Temple of Concord and Victory...but I dare not put them up without your Lordship's illustrious '*Fiat*'."[29]

---

[24] *Loc. cit.* It is possible that these statues were executed by James Lovell. See M. McCarthy, "James Lovell and his Sculptures at Stowe", *The Burlington Magazine*, 115 (1973), 220–232.

[25] James Lovell's receipt for this work is published as Appendix I of McCarthy, *op. cit.*

[26] The cost of the door and windows was £30.12.6 in all. The sashes were not used at the temple in the long run, but were installed at Lord Temple's house in Pall Mall, which was reconstructed and had two rooms added at this time by William Ride. Stowe Papers, Box marked Stowe Repairs 1750–59.

[27] R. Gunnis, *Dictionary of British Sculptors: 1660–1850*, new rev. ed. (London, n.d.), 373.

[28] Stowe Papers, Box marked Stowe Repairs 1760–66.

[29] Letter dated from Stowe, July 5, 1768, among the Lyttelton Manuscripts at Hagley Hall, Worcestershire. I am indebted to Lord Cobham for permission to examine and publish this letter.

By this date, two other important buildings had been erected in the gardens. The more important one, from the point of view of the scale and design of the landscape garden, was the Corinthian Arch (Fig. 6). Situated at the opposite extremity of the estate, it is more than a mile south of the house, and thus represents a doubling of the area that Lord Temple conceived of as his gardens. From the crest of the hill on which it stands, it affords an uninterrupted vista to the south front of the house; or vice-versa, from the south front of the house it directs the spectator's gaze over an uninterrupted sweep of the gardens, apparently to the horizon line. To provide this heroic vista, the gardens of Stowe were drastically altered. The eventual result of the alterations is shown in figure 7, a drawing from the Stowe School Library which may be the preparatory drawing for the engraving of Stowe gardens first published by Seeley of Buckingham in 1797.[30] The basic pattern of the Bridgeman-Kent-Brown gardens remains recognizable, but the double avenue of trees leading to the south front has been felled, and the plantations to either side of that central approach have been severely cut back and irregularized. The lake has been broadened, and the two lake pavilions have been removed from their locations and placed further apart. It was a bold stroke, but everybody who has been to Stowe, or written about it, is agreed as to its triumphant success. Its conception is certainly attributable to Lord Temple, for he wrote in 1762 that he had completed the felling of half of the avenue of trees.[31]

The building of the Corinthian Arch must have been a major factor in determining the form and scale of these landscape alterations. Horace Walpole, in a manuscript note, first named "Mr. T. Pitt" as its architect,[32] and his attribution is confirmed in the Stowe Papers. On 6 November 1765, the builder and carver Edward Batchelor was paid six shillings and three pence, "to $2\frac{1}{2}$ days taking of the Arch and

---

[30] It may also be a copy of that engraving. The name J. C. (or G.) Nattes and the date 1809 have been added at the bottom of the drawing, and the outline of the lake has been altered. These details are published here by kind permission of George Clarke, who brought the drawing to my attention.

[31] Letter of November 21, 1762, addressed to John Wilkes. This was kindly brought to my attention by Michael Gibbon.

[32] The attribution occurs on a note written below Plate I of Walpole's copy of the 1768 *Guide* published by Seeley of Buckingham. This volume is now in the Lewis Walpole Library at Farmington, Connecticut, and I am grateful to Wilmarth S. Lewis for permission to examine it and to publish this note.

Planning the same, and drawing in the House for Mr. Pitt to see."[33] Thomas Pitt (Fig. 8), who was a more important architect than has hitherto been realized, was Lord Temple's cousin. He became Lord Camelford of Boconnoc in Cornwall in 1784.[34]

The plan and elevation of the Corinthian Arch were first published by Seeley of Buckingham in 1765, but the building accounts, which have survived among the Stowe Papers, make it clear that the structure was not finished until 1767. The total cost of the building was £762.7.8½, of which the sculptor James Lovell received £62.19.0 for the carving of the Corinthian capitals and the festoons which ornament the sixty-foot square fabric so proudly.[35] In 1765, Seelye had pointed out that the purpose of the Arch was to create a frame through which the visitor approaching Stowe from Buckingham would see the south front of the mansion for the first time. The arch does this splendidly to this day, and it works equally well as a focus of vision for the visitor surveying the landscape from the portico of the mansion. The 1968 *Guide to Stowe* describes the sight:

> A vista formed by magnificent trees, converging and withdrawing, rolls down to a lake, and up to the skyline beyond, about a mile away. Nothing is formal there; all is idealised landscape. Only three classical buildings provide points of interest: the Corinthian Arch on the crest, and the twin Lake Pavilions below it, backed by dark smudges of yew. These form a restful triangle—revealing incidentally that Stowe did not begin as a fully 'natural' garden, for the good reason that 'natural' gardening virtually began at Stowe.[36]

It is impossible at this point to avoid the question of the relationship between landscape gardening and architecture. To be specific on the subject of Stowe: did the Grecian Temple and the Corinthian Arch

[33] Stowe Papers, Box marked Stowe Repairs 1760–66. Pre-cut stone was supplied by Rowland Jackson, who received £101.17.9, and by Edward Bayliss, who was paid £108.12.1. The builders, Richard Batchelor and his son Edward, were paid £271.1.1 on November 5, 1765, and £57.18.9½ on April 4, 1767.

[34] For an account of Thomas Pitt's works in architecture see H. Colvin, *Biographical Dictionary of English Architects 1660–1840* (London, 1954), 459–60, and M. McCarthy, "The Rebuilding of Stowe House, 1770–1777," *The Huntington Library Quarterly*, May, 1973, 267–298. A biographical account is Sir Tresham Lever, *The House of Pitt* (London, 1947), *passim*.

[35] See McCarthy, "James Lovell", 222–5.

[36] Whistler, Gibbon and Clarke, *Stowe Guide*, 15.

force the opening, softening and serpentining of the plantations? Expressed another way, did neo-classicism in architecture force naturalism in landscape design? Or, as we usually think of it, did the transformation of the gardens dictate the style and scale of the garden buildings? I think it is Horace Walpole who has led us to think that the changes in concepts of the landscape preceded those in architecture, by his categorical statement, à propos William Kent: "We owe the restoration of Greece and the diffusion of architecture to his skill in landscape."[37] But the evidence of the maps of the Stowe estate must give us some misgivings about accepting the order of precedence he established.

Figure 9 is a detail of figure 3, the engraving published by George Bickham to accompany his book, *The Beauties of Stowe*, in 1753. Three years later, Benjamin Seeley published an engraving, a detail of which is figure 10, which shows that the octagonal lake had been irregularized during that period, but that no other changes had taken place. Seeley reprinted this engraving until 1762, then in the following year published a revised state of it, which is reproduced in detail in figure 11. The inner row of the central double avenue of trees had been felled by this date, and the regular canal to the left had gone, to be replaced by turf. Otherwise, the plantations remained very much as Charles Bridgeman had designed them some thirty years earlier. This engraving was republished by Seeley in the 1766 and 1769 editions of the *Guide to Stowe*, but for the edition of 1777 he engraved a new map, shown in detail in figure 12. All the trees of the central avenue had now been felled, and the plantations had been severely cut back. The elaborate *rond-point* to the left had been eliminated, and a comparable simplification of the plantations to the right, the Elysian Fields, had been effected. The double avenue of trees that formerly bound the eastern side of the Elysian Fields had also been felled. There is one other drastic change. The house is now a much more solid block, which reaches forward to the north with its colonnades, and advances a massive six-columned portico to the south.[38] The history of the

[37] Walpole, *Anecdotes*, III, 82.

[38] It should be remembered, in connection with engravings of the Stowe gardens, that they were often sold separately from the *Guides*, and their dates consequently are not necessarily those of the edition of the *Guides* into which they are bound. The best collection of the *Guides* is that in the Stowe School Library, and the dates of engravings given in this paper are based upon a study of that collection made by George Clarke, who generously communicated his findings to me and allowed me permission to publish them here.

rebuilding of the house cannot be entered into here; suffice it to say that the north front was altered from 1770 to 1772, and the south front was completely rebuilt from 1772 to 1777. The architect was Thomas Pitt, in collaboration with Lord Temple, and his designs were based upon elevations devised in the first instance by Robert Adam and James Wyatt.[39]

The result of these alterations was the dominance of the buildings over the landscape. At Stowe the apposition of buildings to each other, the provision of echoing vistas from building to building, determined the form taken by the gardens while Lord Temple lived. Moreover, the concept can certainly be laid to his credit, for it first appeared in the new area of the gardens, the Grecian Valley, begun in 1747 and dominated by the Temple of Concord and Victory, built, as we have seen, under his direction from 1749 to 1763. James Dallaway's appreciation is worth quoting:

> The Temple of Concord and Victory, presiding over so noble a valley, the great arch designed by Mr. T. Pitt, and the smaller in honour of Princess Amelia, disclosing a wonderfully beautiful perspective over the Elysian Fields to the Palladian Bridge and up to the castle on the hill, are monuments of taste, and scenes that I much question if Tempe or Daphne exhibited.[40]

As Dallaway noted, the Doric Arch honouring Princess Amelia (fig. 13), was sited and scaled to frame a vista across the Elysian Fields through the Palladian Bridge to Stowe Castle on the hill beyond Hawkewell Field; in just the same manner as the Corinthian Arch frames the vista across the valley to the south front of the mansion. To quote Hussey, it is "a replica in miniature," and a very successful one.[41] The practiced eye of Horace Walpole, who accompanied the Princess on the occasion of its "opening" in 1768, noted it as "comprehending more beauties of light, shade and buildings, than any picture of Albano I ever saw."[42] Because of the nature of its siting,

[39] See McCarthy, "Stowe House" and "James Lovell."

[40] H. Walpole, *Anecdotes*, with notes by James Dallaway, ed. R. Wornum, II (London, 1849), 693–4, n. 2.

[41] Hussey, *English Gardens*, 110.

[42] Quoted from Whistler, Gibbon and Clarke, *Stowe Guide*, 18.

and because no one has ever yet proposed an architect for the Doric Arch, I suggest he was either Lord Temple or his cousin, Thomas Pitt.

The same reasons prompt me to suggest the same names as architects of the rebuilding of the Palladian Bridge at Stowe. This was a sizeable undertaking. The bridge had existed at least as early as 1742, but not as we see it today. It lay at the south-east extremity of Lord Cobham's gardens, and in keeping with the tightly-enclosed nature of those gardens, its eastern side was closed by a solid wall, which held the relief sculpture, *Britannia Receiving Homage*, by Peter Scheemakers, transferred by William Stephenson to the east pediment of the Temple of Concord and Victory in 1761 (Fig. 5). The Stowe Papers inform us that the London builder, William Ride,[43] sent down a model of a bridge to Stowe in 1760, and it is possible that this was a model of the bridge designed by Lord Pembroke for Wilton, since the Stowe bridge is almost a replica of the Wilton bridge. If this was the bridge mentioned in Ride's bill,[44] then Thomas Pitt can be ruled out as the architect, for he was on the continent from 1760 to 1762; moreover, when he had the opportunity at Hagley to build a Palladian bridge, he departed from the Wilton model, as we shall see. With the opening of the bridge to take in the view of Stowe Castle in the distance, the landscape gardens of Stowe were doubled in extent to the east, as the building of the Corinthian Arch had doubled their extent to the south.[45]

One other garden building at Stowe remains to be considered, the Ladies' Temple, also known as the Queen's Temple. The original was designed by James Gibbs in 1744, and was probably completed in 1747, when William Pain received a series of payments for plastering it.[46] By 1769, it had to serve a double duty, that of answering to Gibbs's Temple of Friendship at the south end of Hawkewell Field, and to Lord Temple's Temple of Concord and Victory on the axis

[43] For an account of William Ride's works in architecture see Colvin, *Dictionary*, 501–2, and McCarthy, "Stowe House."

[44] Stowe Papers, Box marked Stowe Repairs 1750–59. This model, however, may well have been for the Oxford bridge, which, in the absence of a claim by any other architect may also be attributed to Lord Temple. The accounts refer to the "new" bridge, so it may be merely misleading to associate the model with the Palladian bridge. Michael Gibbon has kindly informed me that work on the Oxford bridge began in 1760.

[45] Stowe Castle, however, was probably built twenty years earlier. See Gibbon, "Cobham's Buildings," 214.

[46] Stowe Papers, Box marked Stowe Building and Repair Accounts 1710–47.

of the Grecian Diagonal. It was on the smaller scale and of the more enclosed type of composition that characterized the buildings of Lord Cobham's period, so it did not meet the challenge of the new Temple very successfully. Lord Temple decided to alter it completely. Work began in April of 1772, and a bill presented by Edward Batchelor on December 9 of the following year shows that the fabric was completed, and the balusters set on top it, by that date. James Lovell carved the column and pilaster capitals "of the Composite Order in Portland (stone)," for which he was paid sixty-three pounds in November of 1775. But they were not put into place until summer of 1777, when Edward Batchelor presented his second bill for the Ladies' Temple. The following year Terence Smith was paid for the plasterwork at the building, so its completion can be dated 1778.[47]

The transformation was complete, and the building formed a successful terminus to long Hawkewell Field, fronting it superbly with its four-columned portico raised on a noble flight of steps, answering the four-columned Doric portico of the Temple of Friendship at the far end (Fig. 14). This is the feature, of course, which made it so timely an addition to Stowe gardens, for the alterations gave it the open and predominant character which was consistent with the changes effected in the landscape. They also gave it an element of movement, for just as its portico projects on the south side, so does the semi-circular bow on the north (Fig. 15). Thus it continued to serve as a terminal point at the junction of Hawkewell Field with the Grecian Valley. But it was no longer a full stop; its form invited the spectator to go around and beyond it. The semi-circular bow on the first floor of the north elevation is open, and is sustained by Ionic columns, in response to the order of the Temple of Concord and Victory.

The Stowe Papers do not allow us to identify the architect of the new Ladies' Temple positively. Modern scholars have favoured a French architect, Georges-François Blondel. Very little is known of him, except that in 1774 he wrote to Sir William Chambers, complaining that Lord Temple had not paid him for several designs, one of which he mentions as having been made for the Ladies' Temple. That would seem to settle the matter, were it not that Blondel's

[47] Stowe Papers, Box marked Stowe Repairs 1767–74, and Box marked Stowe Repairs 1775–93.

claims on Lord Temple can be shown to be unfounded in several respects, so there is no particular reason to believe that the design for the Ladies' Temple was that which he submitted.[48] The other architect who has been proposed is Vincenzo Valdré, but he did not arrive in England until two years after the start of the building, and there is no evidence to suggest that he was engaged at Stowe until after Lord Temple's death in 1779.[49] However, there seems to be no good reason to deny an attribution to Thomas Pitt. The architect of Stowe House was certainly capable of designing the Ladies' Temple, and there are obvious points of comparison between the two buildings. The most telling, in our context, is the "movement" that each displays, to use Robert Adam's term,[50] the sense that they give of having been designed specifically to harmonize with their landscape setting, the evolution of which we have examined earlier.

To summarize the conclusions of that examination will be useful. Lord Temple played a major part in the creation of the first "natural" landscape in England, the Grecian Valley, from 1747 to 1763. He extended the concepts involved in that creation to the gardens south of the house, slowly from 1753 to 1769, and rapidly from 1769 to 1777, when the gardens assumed their final form. Perhaps the most important corollary to this examination is its creation of doubt as to the importance and originality of Lancelot Brown. As we have seen, he left Stowe gardens two years after the beginning of the Grecian Valley. There is no evidence that he ever returned there, yet he, rather than Lord Temple, has been given credit for the creation of Stowe gardens, and thereby for the creation of the natural English landscape.[51] This attribution will not stand investigation on the basis of our present knowledge. As I mentioned earlier, George Clarke has established the importance of Lord Cobham, William Pitt, and their close relations, including Lord Temple, to the development of the pre-1749 gardens of Stowe. I have sought to establish the importance of Lord Temple

[48] J. Harris, "Blondel at Stowe," *Connoisseur*, 163 (1964), 173–6. For the case against Blondel's authorship, and further information on that architect's relations with Lord Temple, see McCarthy, "Stowe House."

[49] For Vincenzo Valdré's work at Stowe see M. Gibbon, "A Forgotten Italian at Stowe," *Country Life*, 160 (1966), 260–3, and McCarthy, "Stowe House."

[50] For an analysis of "movement" in the works of the Adam brothers, see J. Lees-Milne, *The Age of Adam* (London, 1947), 71.

[51] The most recent example is E. Hyams, *Capability Brown and Humphry Repton* (London, 1971), 22.

and his cousin Thomas Pitt. Clearly, Lancelot Brown's conception of landscaping owed much to these amateur architects and landscape designers, and it is probably more correct to see him as the popularizer of the style developed by them at Stowe, rather than to see him as an innovator in landscape gardening. It might be objected that Brown could have given his employers their original ideas before he left Stowe gardens in 1749, particularly since the Grecian Valley was started two years earlier. But that does **not** seem probable, for Brown had neither the learning, nor the experience gained in travel and commerce with artists, that the lords of Stowe had. Nor did his later architecture reveal any of the largeness of conception and facility of manner that theirs did; it provides no reason to suppose that his ability in design was exceptionally strong, let alone original.

The validity of this reading of the progress of landscape design in the eighteenth century can be pointed up by examining Hagley Park (Fig. 16) in Worcestershire. The most prestigious estate of the mid-eighteenth century, after that of Stowe, it was the property of Lord Temple's cousin and correspondent, Lord George Lyttelton. When we reflect that this landscape and its buildings were also created by amateurs, we must wonder why we have forgotten Horace Walpole's judgement that: "Gardening and architecture owe as much to the nobility and to men of fortune as to the professors."[52] Hagley Park has never been ascribed to any professional architect or landscape designer, and in view of the close association of Stowe with Hagley, there is every probability Lord Temple's advice was sought and heeded in its creation. The date of the start of work at Hagley cannot be determined exactly, but the Park received its form certainly in the final years of the 1740's—that is, the years of the creation of the Grecian Valley at Stowe. Now we know that Lord Temple's brother-in-law, William Pitt, later Lord Chatham (Fig. 17) was a constant visitor to Stowe and to Hagley, and we know that he had a great reputation as a designer of landscapes. We have seen the brothers-in-law invited to Gosfield Hall to lay out the gardens there. It is probably impossible, and unnecessary, to separate the influence of one from that of the other in the case of Stowe, but it is safe to say that William Pitt exerted greater influence in matters relating to the shaping of the landscape at Hagley.

[52] H. Walpole, *Anecdotes*, IV (London, 1771), 150–1.

The new landscape park at Hagley, like the new mansion house. was a product of the deliberations of a Committee of Taste. Contemporary records afford us occasional glimpses of their deliberations. George Lyttelton wrote, for example, to Sanderson Miller on June 1, 1749: "I have consulted Mr. Pitt upon cutting down the trees behind the Rotunda, or planting evergreens as you propose, but he don't think it advicable to venture upon either, unless upon very mature consideration. I shall see how it looks when I go down in August, & it will be time enough then to decide. I have at last got a Plan for my Seat from his Cousin, but cant yet obtain the Elevation; however, I hope I shall have it soon, for I wont let him rest till I have."[53]

Conveniently, this letter brings together the two amateur architects principally responsible for the garden buildings of Hagley. Mr. Pitt's cousin was John Pitt of Encombe in Dorset, "the Commoner of the West." Since Sir Thomas Lyttelton was still alive at this date, and for a further two years, and since the site of the new Hagley Hall was still in doubt in 1753,[54] it is surprising that writers on Sanderson Miller's work at Hagley should have understood the reference in this letter to "my Seat" to refer to plans for the new mansion house.[55] The date and context point clearly to a garden seat, and it is probable that the semi-octagonal building, known as Thomson's Seat in honour of the author of *The Seasons*, is the building in question. An attribution of this building, and of the Rotunda at Hagley, to John Pitt exists in the hand of George Lyttelton himself.[56] The Rotunda can be seen in figure 16. We find from contemporary letters that it was of the Ionic order, that its dome was of stone "with thin lead underneath to keep out wet," and that it cost two hundred pounds.[57] George Lyttelton's letters to Sanderson Miller reveal further that the stones of the columns varied in colour, and for that reason Miller's mason, William Hitchcox, who undoubtedly built it under the direction of Sanderson Miller, suggested that the columns should be painted.[58]

Another name needs to be mentioned in connection with the laying out of Hagley's landscape park, that of Miss Molly West, affection-

[53] Warwick County Records Office, CR 125B/348.
[54] M. Williams, *Letters of William Shenstone* (London, 1939), 384.
[55] Dickins and Stanton, *Correspondence*, 283; Wood and Hawkes, "Sanderson Miller," 110.
[56] G. W. Beard and J. H. Folkes, "John Chute and Hagley Hall," *The Architectural Review*, 112 (1952), 200.
[57] T. Hull, *Select Letters*, I (London, 1778), 95.
[58] Warwick County Records Office, CR 125B/350.

ately addressed as "Dear Dryad" by her cousin, George Lyttelton, in their correspondence, which survives among the Lyttelton manuscripts at Hagley Hall. An important letter for our purposes, in that it confirms the date of the major alterations, is that of 29 March 1748, which entrusts the Dryad of Hagley with the planting of trees about the cottage and the pool. It is also important in that it shows that the disposition of the trees had previously been determined by William Pitt, who was about to visit Hagley: "He will be much disappointed not to see it done, and so indeed shall I, much more than at the delay of the Rotunda.... However, I dare say you do all you can for our satisfaction, and we must be content with the grand work of the Castle."[59]

The castle, of course, was Sanderson Miller's Gothic eye-catcher and prospect-tower, the first of many such follies which he designed, and one which is still standing.[60] No visual evidence of the form of the cottage remains, but it is reasonable to suppose that this too was designed by Sanderson Miller, because we know that Hitchcox built it.[61] Miller also designed the Doric Dairy built from 1752, and described by George Lyttelton as "altogether the most agreeable building I have." Again, we lack visual evidence of the building, but the correspondence informs us that its walls were thick, and that it had four windows of red and blue glass, though, alas, the coloured glass featuring birds and other animals, which Lady Lyttelton dearly wanted could not be found.[62] However, the next Doric building at Hagley survives, a landmark in every sense of the word. Designed by James Stuart in 1758, it was erected the following year. It has not yet been

[59] I am grateful to Viscount Cobham of Hagley Hall for permission to examine this letter.

[60] A list of Sanderson Miller's Gothic garden buildings will be found in Wood and Hawkes, "Sanderson Miller," 108–10. One correction to that list can be made. The ruinated castle at Wimpole, Cambridgeshire, was not erected by Miller, but by James Essex, in consultation with Lancelot Brown, in 1768. This appears from two letters written by James Barton, steward of the second Lord Hardwicke, to James Essex. Their location is British Museum, Add. MSS. 6771, fol. 99 verso, and fol. 178 verso. The print of the castle at Wimpole that hangs in Radway Grange was sent to Miller as a present as late as 1777, as Warwick County Record Office, CR 125B/72 shows. Correspondence between George Lyttelton and Sanderson Miller on the subject of this building has been published in Dickins and Stanton, *Correspondence*, 271–2. It can be supplemented by one of the few extant letters written by Miller, and so far unnoticed, British Museum, Add. MSS. 35769, (Hardwicke Papers CCCXXI), fol. 55.

[61] This is evident from the letter of George Lyttelton to Miss West, quoted in part above, p. 51.

[62] Warwick County Records Office, CR 125B/631, 356, 359, listed in chronological order.

pointed out that the executive architect of this harbinger of the Greek Revival in European architecture was Sanderson Miller. This is clear, however, from the postscript of a letter he received from George (now Lord) Lyttelton, of March 17th, 1759: "I don't know whether Mr. Stuart has yet sent the Drawings for the Capitals, Freize, etc. of the Dorick Building: but I believe Hitchcox has one for all the plain and solid parts. The brick which it is to be lined with should be carried from the old house at such times as the cart can be conveniently spared."[63]

The next of the garden buildings at Hagley was designed by the amateur who was responsible for so much of the grandeur of Stowe, Thomas Pitt, nephew to Lord Lyttelton. Between the time of his return from the continent in 1762 and the visit of Richard Pococke to Hagley in 1764, he designed the Palladian bridge at Hagley. It is not mentioned in the correspondence of the period, apart from Pococke's unpublished notice. But fortunately there has recently come to light a drawing by the Reverend Thomas Streatfeild, which can be identified with some confidence as a view towards the Palladian bridge in Hagley park (Fig. 18).[64] This drawing, first exhibited at the Sabin Galleries, London, in November 1971, shows a bridge smaller than those at Wilton, Stowe and Prior Park, for it has no more than three bays equally accented. This would lead us to doubt its identification, were it not for the description given by that accurate and indefatigable observer of buildings, Richard Pococke, Bishop of Ossorry: "Built after young Mr. Pitt's design, L. Lyttelton's nephew, of the old Ionic order with something particular in the [volute (?)] of the Capital. The balustrade rises from the plinth its proper heighth without touching either the base or the shaft; which execution is singular."[65]

[63] Warwick County Records Office, CR 125B/365. For the importance of this building see N. Pevsner, "The Doric Revival," *Studies in Art, Architecture and Design*, I (London, 1968), 203. For the importance of Sanderson Miller's contribution to the Greek Revival, see M. McCarthy, "Documents on the Greek Revival in Architecture," *The Burlington Magazine*, 114 (1972), 760–9.

[64] I am indebted to Mr. John Harris, Curator of Drawings at the Royal Institute of British Architects, London, for having brought this drawing to my attention, and for suggesting that it might be a drawing of the Hagley bridge. Mr. William Drummond, of the Sabin Galleries, London, kindly made the drawing available to me for study before the exhibition. The identification of the bridge as that of Hagley has now been accepted. See M. Binney, "Country Houses on View," *Country Life*, 150 (1971), 1259.

[65] British Museum, Add. MSS. 14260, fol. 177.

The particularity of the capitals cannot be discerned in the draw-ing, even with magnification, but the independence of the columns from the balustrade is clearly visible (Fig. 19). Pitt did not erect the columns on stone piers the same height as the balustrade—as Lord Pembroke had done—but on small stone slabs. This allowed for an interesting interplay between the columns and the balusters, and gave the building a more light and graceful air. It is important to note that this design is more true to the Palladian prototype, the design for the Rialto bridge in Venice. Hagley's Palladian bridge is thus, with the Doric pavilion of James Stuart, a witness to the scholarly approach to design that characterized the best of the garden buildings of the period.[66]

So much for the garden buildings at Hagley. Very little can be said about the designing of the landscape itself. No evidence of earth-moving has come to light, and it is vain to seek plans for alterations from professional hands. A visitor to Hagley in 1768 was Lady Temple of Stowe, who had reason to know all about changes in landscape design. She wrote of its

> Every lawn and every grove,
> That decked by Nature's hand alone,
> To Kent or Brown was never known.[67]

Though it is something of an anti-climax after the splendours of Eastbury, Stowe and Hagley, it is appropriate to conclude this paper by looking at the garden of the amateur architect who contributed so much to the great gardens of England, Thomas Pitt, Lord Camelford of Boconnoc in Cornwall. There is very little to tell. Accounts in the Cornwall Record Office show that a "New Garden" was begun in

---

[66] Hussey, *English Gardens*, 49–52, gives a history of Palladian bridges in England, but he assumes that the bridge at Hagley was a repetition of the design of Lord Pembroke's bridge at Wilton, copied with variations at Stowe and at Prior Park. It should be noted that Thomas Whately records a fifth Palladian bridge, that at Wotton, another landscape designed by Lord Temple and his circle, and one which merits the particular praise of that admirable author. See Whately, *Observations*, 89–93. With reference to the lack of visual evidence of the appearance of Hagley Park and its buildings, contemporary writers suggest that the scandal of the separation of Lord Lyttelton from his second wife in 1756 made Hagley an unpopular place for visiting, despite its fame in the years immediately preceding this. See M. Wyndham, *Chronicles of the Eighteenth Century*, II (London, 1924), 271–3. The subsequent notoriety of the second Lord Lyttelton cannot have improved matters. The remark is attrib-uted to him that a classical garden is as ridiculous an expression as a classical plum-pudding. See T. Frost, *The Life of Thomas Lord Lyttelton* (London, 1876), 313–5.

[67] Quoted from D. Stroud, *Capability Brown* (London, 1950), 31.

March, 1770, and that its cost to the end of 1772 was £239.11.2. In 1773 a park fence was added, which cost £122.5.10.[68] However, the only garden building recorded is an obelisk to the memory of Sir Richard Lyttelton, of which there is a drawing by Sir John Soane, who repaired it after it had been struck by lightning in 1787. Thomas Pitt had big aspirations for the embellishment of his family estate, however, and he wrote to his executive architect and friend, John Soane, on 7 July 1787: "You know I gave you a sketch of a *Château en Espagne* that will never be executed."[69] He did in fact add a wing to Boconnoc House, but we must suppose that the drawing by Thomas Pitt for an entrance arch to Boconnoc, which partly survives in Sir John Soane's Museum (Fig. 20), is a detail of the unexecuted castle in Spain.

If this drawing does nothing else, it explains to us why Edward Batchelor was paid six shillings and three pence for drawing out the Corinthian arch at Stowe for Mr. Pitt, in 1765. As an exercise in architectural draughtsmanship, it is lamentable. But it is a mistake to expect amateur architects to display excellence in drawing. The mentor of the age, Lord Chesterfield, had advised them that this skill was beneath the dignity of their station in life.[70] For Thomas Pitt, this lesson was reinforced by his uncle, William, who wrote him while he was an undergraduate at Cambridge, forbidding his indulgence in the pleasure of drawing.[71]

It was part of the duty of their station in life, however, to provide their age with standards of taste, invention, and scholarship. I hope that this examination of their contributions to the principal gardens of England has demonstrated that in the art of landscape gardening, no less than in that of architecture, they were the innovators whose works inspired those of the professionals.

All quotations from the Stowe Papers are made possible by kind permission of the Trustees of the Henry E. Huntington Library and Art Gallery, San Marino, California, and by the

[68] Cornwall County Records Office, Papers of Captain T.D.G. Fortescue, D.D.F. 188.

[69] The correspondence relating to Soane's work at Boconnoc and other properties of Lord Camelford is in Sir John Soane's Museum, London, and is quoted here by kind permission of the Trustees of Sir John Soane's Museum. The drawing of the entrance arch for Boconnoc is among the Soane-Pitt letters. That of the obelisk is in an album marked *Original Sketches*, fol. 127. I am grateful to Sir John Summerson for the second reference.

[70] Lord Chesterfield, *An Essay on Design* (London, 1749), 62–3.

[71] Lord Grenville, ed., *Letters from Lord Chatham* (London, 1804), Letter 3, dated from Bath, January 12, 1754.

the co-operation of the Department of Manuscripts of the Huntington Library. I owe particular thanks to Miss Anne Caiger, Assistant Archivist, who placed the relevant manuscripts at my disposal for study. Professor Sir Nikolaus Pevsner kindly advised me in the preparation and writing of this paper, and George Clarke, Michael Gibbon and Kenneth Woodbridge made many helpful corrections to an earlier version of it. My research was conducted intermittently over a two-year period, and I am grateful to The Canada Council, the Office of Research Administration of the University of Toronto, and the Travel Fund of the Faculty of Education of the University of Toronto, for financial assistance in pursuing it. Gratitude is due also to the suppliers of the illustrations, who are mentioned in the captions below the plates.

Sir Uvedale Price
and the Picturesque Garden:
the Evidence of the Coleorton Papers

MARCIA ALLENTUCK

I

While Sir Uvedale Price was not the first critic in the history of British eighteenth century aesthetic theory to write about the picturesque and its relation to the fine and useful arts, he was the concept's most discerning, sensible, evocative, and influential explicator. As art historians and architectural historians, we can still learn much from the dialectic in Price's writings between accident and order, between emotion and principles, as he applied it to his analyses of the picturesque, and from his independent refusal to succumb to the fallacies of contemporary historicism in practice and theory.

"There are few words," Price wrote in the first edition (1794) of *An Essay on the Picturesque, as Compared with the Sublime and the Beautiful: and on the Use of Studying Pictures for the Purpose of Improving Real Landscape*,[1] "whose meaning has been less accurately determined than that of the word Picturesque. In general, I believe, it is applied to every object, and every kind of scenery, which has been, or might be represented with good effect in painting... But, considered as a separate character, it has never yet been accurately distinguished from the sublime and the beautiful." It was Price's calculated and consistent insistence upon the character of the picturesque as "not less separate and distinct than either the sublime and the

[1] London, 1794. Unless otherwise indicated, all quotations in this lecture will be from this edition, in which Price's thoughts are fresh and not expanded or over-elaborated, as they sometimes are in the editions of 1796–1798 and 1810. As I have no facsimile fever, being solely concerned with the legitimate comforts of the modern reader, I shall also normalize Price's unpublished writings wherever necessary in terms of spelling, punctuation, &c., whenever quoting from them.

beautiful,"upon its "variety and intricacy," its "sudden and broken" lines and surfaces, as opposed to the "smoothness" of beauty, with its "absolute equality of uniformity of surface" and "flowing lines" that set off the picturesque. Thus, Price argued, "I am therefore persuaded that the two opposite qualities of roughness, and of sudden variation, joined to that of irregularity, are the most efficient causes of the picturesque."

Just as the picturesque is separated from the beautiful, proceeded Price, so

> it is equally distinct from the sublime; for though there are some qualities common to them both, yet they differ in many essential points and proceed from very different causes. In the first place, greatness of dimension is a powerful cause of the sublime; the picturesque has no connection with dimensions of any kind (in which it differs from the beautiful also) and is as often found in the smallest as in the largest objects.—The sublime being founded on principles of awe and terror, never descends to anything light or playful; the picturesque... is equally adapted to the grandest and to the gayest scenery.—Infinity is one of the most efficient causes of the sublime; the boundless ocean... inspires awful sensations: to give it picturesqueness you must destroy that cause of its sublimity; for it is on the shape and disposition of its boundaries that the picturesque in great measure must depend.

Neither the Burkean uniformity of sublime terror nor astonishment was deemed by Price relevant to the picturesque, whose effect was

> curiosity; an effect which, though less splendid and powerful, has a more general influence; it neither relaxes nor violently stretches the fibres, but by its active agency keeps them to their full tone, and... when mixed with either of the other characters, corrects the languor of beauty, or the horror of sublimity. But as the nature of every corrective must be to take off from the peculiar effect of what it is to correct, so does the picturesque when united to either of the others. It is the coquetry of nature; it makes beauty

more amusing, more varied, more playful... by its variety, its intricacy, its partial concealments, it excites the active curiosity which gives play to the mind, loosening those iron bonds with which astonishment chains up its faculties.

It is clear here that, in modern terms, Price treats the picturesque as a therapeutic, rather than an aesthetic force primarily; in eighteenth century terms, to be sure, he is a close follower of Du Bos and David Hume in his emphasis on "play to the mind."

Although concentrating always on the "separate character" of the picturesque, Price was not a rigid categorizer, but a pragmatic one:

> Where characters, however distinct in their nature, are perpetually mixed together in such various degrees and manners, it is not always easy to draw the exact line of separation: I think, however, we may conclude, that where an object, or a set of objects, is without smoothness or grandeur, but from its intricacy, its sudden and irregular deviations, its variety of forms, tints, and lights and shadows, is interesting to a cultivated eye, it is simply picturesque; such, for instance, are the rough banks that often inclose a bye-road or a hollow lane [Fig. 1]: Imagine the size of these banks and the space between them to be increased till the lane becomes a deep dell,—the coves large caverns,—the peeping stones hanging rocks, so that the whole may impress an idea of awe and grandeur;— the sublime will then be mixed with the picturesque [Fig. 2], though the scale only, not the style of the scenery, would be changed. On the other hand, if parts of the banks were smooth and gently sloping,—or the middle space a soft, close-bitten turf,—or if a gentle stream passed between them, whose clear unbroken surfaces reflected all their varieties,—the beautiful and the picturesque, by means of that softness and smoothness, would then be united.... [Fig. 3].

"Of the three characters," Price summed up, "two only are in any degree subject to the improver; to *create* the sublime is above our contracted powers, though we may sometimes heighten and at all times lower its effects by art. It is, therefore, on a proper attention to the beautiful and the picturesque, that the art of improving the landscape must depend."[2]

Upon these basic observations by Price, numerous aestheticians, artists, improvers, and travellers rang a multitude of changes. My concern will be with two phrases of immense importance used by Price in these passages: "interesting to the cultivated eye," and "the art of improving landscape." In view of the significance of these phrases for the understanding of the picturesque and its arch-promulgator, it is indeed surprising that there has never been a critical biography of Price, nor an annotated edition of his seminal works— not even an edition of his extant letters is available. To remedy these deficiencies, I have for some time been engaged in this three-pronged project, and in the course of my research, I have turned up much unpublished material. I wish to share with you some results of this research. As I have had to adhere to a strict principle of selection, I have chosen to concentrate upon the only collection of Price's manuscripts to be found in America, which I have just completed editing. The collection consists of one hundred and six letters from Sir Uvedale Price (Fig. 4) and his wife, Lady Caroline, to the connoisseur, patron of the arts, picturesque painter and landscaper, Sir George Beaumont, and his wife Margaret. Written during the period 1794–1828, these letters comprise the bulk of the Coleorton Papers and come from Coleorton Hall, Sir George's estate in Leicestershire. Price helped Beaumont enlarge Coleorton Hall architecturally according to picturesque principles, and to landscape according to the "separate character" (28 November 1794) of the picturesque tenets of the "broken and varied" (24 August 1804) and the "rugged and abrupt." (28 November 1794) The aim was always to create striking effects, especially a "painter's broken foreground." (10 July 1804) "We have the same pursuits, the same tastes," Price wrote to Beaumont (10 August 1811).

The Coleorton Papers are now at the Pierpont Morgan Library, and I must here express my thanks to the Director and the Trustees for reserving them for my use, and to Mr. Herbert Cahoon, Curator of Manuscripts, for his steady co-operation during the complicated process of preparing them for publication.

[2] Price, *Essay*, 34, 36, 43–45, 80–81, 86–88, and 90.

The Price letters (the Beaumont half of the correspondence is lost) show the variegated interests of their author, and each one offers proof positive of the man's radical psychological well-being, his lack of posturing and pretense, his generosity in friendship, his capacity for joy in the three major preoccupations of his life, in his words—"pictures, scenery... music." (11 March 1823) His strong interests in other areas such as Whig politics, the theatre, and classical studies are no less evident. He was worldly but not superficial, confident but not smug. Couched in easy, rapid, witty, incisive prose, leavened by countless quotations in Latin, Greek, French, and Italian, the letters underscore Price's ability to see himself realistically, and to accept what he sees, without heroics or embarrassment, but with humour and with legitimate strength of ego.

Despite his healthy outlook, financial security, and spirited life, Price was highly accident prone, and a great valetudinarian; his accounts of unrelenting journeys in search of the picturesque whilst in the grip of acute attacks of rheumatism, hemorrhoids, or dyspepsia speak positively for the pursuit of an obsession. Even in his last years he was undaunted by a severe injury to an eye from a protruding tree branch—"from my constant warfare with boughs," he told Beaumont on 27 October 1816. This accident was in due course to leave him with clouded vision: "It is *not* recover'd, nor even likely to recover," he wrote of his eye, "it *was* the strongest of the two, it *is* the weakest; it used to see clearly; it now sees everything as through a mist; letters, whether in print or writing, all dance..." Thus he wrote poignantly in the seventieth year of his life of the atrophy of his visual capacity—his visual sensibility was with him until the end: "Excepting you, and very few others, no one takes such unceasing pleasure and interest in everything visible as I did." (17 September 1816)

Price was hardly numb to the cruel irony of circumstance in this respect, as he was always more concerned with vision than association, insisting not upon the innocent but the self-conscious, the disciplined, even the synaesthetic eye—for what is picturesque preoccupation with rough surfaces but a species of synaesthesia? "The sight takes so many lessons from the touch," he informed Beaumont, "that it soon grows quicker in distinguishing them than its master, and from sympathy receives the same kind of sensations from them." (4 December 1794)

After immersion in Price's synaesthetic explications and examples, both published and unpublished, one must find Bernard Berenson's "tactile values" highly derivative.[3]

II

Price's "cultivated eye," during the eighty-two years of an immensely active and satisfying life, was never satiated. It could be sustained, nourished, and stimulated, according to these letters, by diverse works of man and nature. It was not only what man could manipulate to rise from out the earth, but what he could create to work above it that intrigued Price. For example, he plans avidly with their mutual friend, the aesthetician and landscaper, Richard Payne Knight (he reports to Beaumont on 5 September 1797) to go to Coalbrookdale in Shropshire to see the elegantly fluid tracery of the cast iron bridge (Figs. 5, 6)—the first to use this material—spanning the River Severn. Designed in 1775–1779 by Thomas Farnolls Pritchard, a Shrewsbury architect, cast at Abraham Darby's Madeley Iron Works, it was soon to be the inspirer of memorable drawings, paintings, and engravings by George Robertson, James Fittler, Michael Angelo Rooker, William Ellis, Matthew Dubourg, and Francis Chesham, among others. It is instructive to note that it was after this expedition that Price added the section on bridges (pp. 327–345 particularly) to the expansion of the second edition of his *Essay*, the first volume of which had appeared in 1796. In the second volume of this second edition, which was published in 1798,[4] Price included this section in his new division, "Essay on Architecture and Buildings," wherein he considered buildings as connected with scenery, and functioning in accordance with it, or, indeed, in the country, "in some degree subordinate and dependant" on it.[5] After emphasizing that the "architect of buildings in the country should be *architetto pittore*, for indeed he ought not only have the mind, but the hand of a painter; not only to be acquainted with the principles, but, as far as design goes, with the practice of landscape painting," Price embarked on a

---

[3] Cf. *Aesthetics and History* (Garden City, 1948), especially 69–73 *passim*.
[4] Hereford, 1798.
[5] Passages quoted are on pp. 206–208, 214, and 219.

long disquisition on several of his favourite subjects. Included were his strong animadversions against "Capability" Brown and his followers (Humphry Repton understood): "...there is a strong repugnance...in him who has studied Titian, Claude, and Poussin, and the style of art and of nature that they had studied, to copy the clumps, the naked canals, and no less naked buildings of Mr. Brown... the Genius of the *bare and bald*...cannot take up a house from the midst of its decorations, and place it in a meadow, [yet] he has often made all decorations vanish, and a meadow appear in their place." (Fig. 7).[6] There were no reservations, however, in Price's disquisition on bridges which "in every style of scenery...are objects of the most interesting kind: whether we consider their great and obvious utility, and the almost intrinsic beauty of their forms; or their connection with the most pleasing scenes in nature, and the charms which they add to water, and receive from it in return....when all the circumstances of an arched bridge over a broad and rapid river, from the foundation to the last finishing, are considered, it may be reckoned among the noblest efforts of architecture; uniting, perhaps, in a higher degree than any other building, beauty, grandeur, utility, and real, as well as apparent difficulty of execution." It is in the discussion of bridges after seeing Coalbrookdale, that Price acknowledged an occasion when the calculated pursuit of the man-made picturesque could be transcended legitimately by the grandeur of simplicity. "The situation of a bridge most commonly confers on it such distinction, that it wants no ornaments to mark it, and to detach it from other objects: then the arches themselves form such grand and beautiful opening, that they require no artificial breaks or embellishments, to disguise or adorn them; and their natural arrangement, is as simple and beautiful as their form." But he immediately restored the picturesque in a different aspect—the aspect of motion: "The peculiarity of situation, from which a bridge seems, as it were, to pass from one

---

[6] The Coleorton Papers are replete with favourable references to Claude and negative judgements of Brown. "I love such chaste and genuine nature as we see in Claude," he told Lady Beaumont (2 February 1795); but of his impending visit to Ashburnham he complained to Sir George: "I am afraid the *Genius of the bare and bold* has been very busy with his scythe all round the Mansion,; if I may judge from a view I saw of it the other day, among many other vile prints of places; it is taken so, that you look across the water to the house directly in front...it is indeed shaven... The worst is that Brown fixes and stamps such a character of monotony on all he does, that the two great correctors, Time and Accident, can do little or nothing towards changing it..." (24 July 1812)

side of a river to another, with something analogous to motion," he admits, "may appear fantastic, (but) will, I believe, lead to very just principles."[7] Although Price attributed the quality of beauty to the massiveness of stone bridges, and the picturesque quality of intricacy to those of wood, it is clear that the iron bridge at Coalbrookdale with its unembellished piers would call forth in Price the empathetic feeling of grandeur, for which the picturesque tracery of the iron would be seasoning. What would unite these two characters of the beautiful and the picturesque would be motion, and it is significant that in a letter of 28 January 1798 to Beaumont, he commented:

> I am particularly glad that you are struck with what I have said about the idea of motion in a bridge [Price frequently sent his manuscript drafts to Beaumont for editorial comments] as there is always some risk in that sort of idea, which requires some better sanction than the author's own paternal fondness. Charles Fox read it without making any objection: as to praise or approbation, he rarely bestows any at the time, but perhaps three or four months hence when you would suppose he had forgot every thing about it, he may say, if he happen to think so,—You were quite right about that ideal motion in bridges; & then will canvas the whole subject. I have just seen Nash the architect, & he was struck just as you were, & told me he had mentioned it to Repton, not as an idea of mine but as something he had lately read in a book; & he told me Repton was also very much delighted with it....

In his emphasis upon simplicity in bridges, Price implied the same kind of caveat as he did in the second edition of his *Essay*, when he spoke of Boucher as a painter who had "overshot the mark...he seems to have collected together all the singularly abrupt and irregular forms that he had ever seen, in order to be superlatively picturesque..."[8] This condemnation of Boucher's "abuse" of the picturesque follows Price's discussion of bridges by only a few pages (Fig. 8).

In the Coleorton Papers, however, when he turned to descriptions of the Devil's Bridge in his favourite part of North Wales, he un-

[7] *Essay* (1798), 327, 330, 332–334.
[8] *Essay* (1798), 365.

questionably delighted in the mixed mode of what he dubbed "the sublime of intricacy,"[9] where the intricacy of the scenery, intrinsically picturesque, could contribute as well to sublimity. He urged the Welsh wonder, the Devil's Bridge, consisting of two arches, one dating from the eleventh-twelfth centuries, and the upper from the eighteenth, upon Beaumont, as Price's summer home, Castle House, built by John Nash at Aberystwyth and situated within full view of the ruins of Aberystwyth Castle, was very close (Figs. 11, 12). "With regard to your particular motives for having a house in Wales, the Devil's Bridge with its cascades, one of the most surprisingly romantic scenes in all the principality, is within twelve miles on a fast turnpike road. Knight raves about it, and I have had such delight in exploring...& [making] communications to the depths and chasms." (18 March 1798) A more detailed account of the bridge may be found in the narrative of Price's contemporary, the picturesque traveller, J. T. Barber:

> In a few paces [we] found ourselves on the bridge, suspended over a gulph at which even recollection shudders. This bridge bestrides a lane of almost perpendicular rocks, patched with wood, whose summits are here scarcely five yards asunder. At a terrific depth in the glen rages unseen the impetuous Mynach, engulphed between protruding crags and pendant foliage.... it leaves the imagination free to all the terrors of concealed danger.... Nor is the singular appearance of these arches devoid of picturesque effect: being tastefully besprinkled with verdure, and relieved by the intervention of numerous branchy trees: while the naked black opposing cliffs, worn out into curious hollows by the torrents, exhibit as bold and rocky a chasm as ever was traced by the pencil of Salvator.[10]

Not only bridges but castles as well absorbed Price, as later revisions of his *Essay* showed: they demonstrated to his satisfaction that, while "succession and uniformity, when united to greatness of dimension, are among the most efficient causes of grandeur in buildings, yet causes of a very opposite nature...often tend to produce the same

---

[9] *Essay* (1798), 258.
[10] U. Price, *A Tour Throughout South Wales* (London, 1803), 111–113.

effects. These are, the accumulation of unequal, and, at least, apparently irregular forms, and the intricacy of their disposition." (Fig. 14) By making intricacy a cause of grandeur, he elevated the picturesque mode: "The forms, and the disposition of some of the old castles built on eminences, fully illustrate what I have just advanced: the different outworks and massive gateways; towers rising behind towers; the main body perhaps rising higher than them all, and on one side descending in one immense solid wall... all impress grand and awful ideas."[11] When these edifices were in ruins, so much the better for picturesque effects. Price was persistent in urging Sir George to paint landscapes in such Welsh surroundings and in acquiring them: "How has painting gone on since I saw you? Have you finished any of the pictures we looked over together just before we left town and which you meant to send into the country for that purpose? I am particularly anxious about two of them as I am positively to have one of them at least. I have them both in my eye, and should be amazingly puzzled which to choose: that of Conway Castle is the most striking, and from having seen the original so much with you I feel a particular interest in the subject." (13 January 1805)

As we shall see, Price exerted no less care in improving his estate, Foxley, according to picturesque criteria than he did in constructing his Welsh summer home to harmonize with its surrounding scenery; truly he consulted the genius of the place before he directed John Nash's work. While in process of advising Beaumont about Coleorton, he wrote on 18 March 1798 to thank him for prompt payment for a large order of Herefordshire cider which he had earlier sent him, and confessed:

> Though you and I hate the whole subject of debtor and creditor from the bottom of our souls, in these pinching times one must think of it. Here I am pinched and squeezed because forsooth I must take a fancy for building at Aberystwyth! I did resist as long as I could. I believe at least two years after I had got the ground, but Lady Caroline and I found ourselves always on the spot, always looking at the waves breaking against the near-rocks, and at the long chain of distant mountains with their monarch Snowdon at their head

[11] *Essay* (1798), 336.

[Fig. 13], and we thought how charming it would be [to] look at it comfortably from our own window in all weathers... just when the waves are the most magnificent: and I must say we have enjoyed it even more than I expected. At first I thought merely of running up two or three nutshells of rooms, and got a plan from a common Welsh carpenter: then Nash was mentioned to me, and he had a mind to build me a larger house indeed, but a square bit of architecture. I told him however that I must have, not only some of the *windows,* but some of the *rooms* turned to particular points, and that he must arrange it in his best manner: I explained to him the reasons why I built it so close to the rock, shewed him the effect of the broken foreground and its varied line, and how by that means the foreground was connected with the rocks in the second ground; all which would be lost by placing the house further back. He was excessively struck with these reasons which he said he had never thought of before in the most distant degree, and he has I think contrived the house most admirably for the situation, and the form of it is certainly extremely varied from my having obliged him to turn the rooms to different aspects.

This house constituted one of Nash's earliest experiments in relating a building to its surroundings. In it, Nash produced a structure of odd but exciting aspect, a stuccoed villa in a quasi-Gothic style, which exploited the view of the sea in three directions. This castellated structure possessed octagonal towers at the corners, and canopied balconies; the edifice corresponded to Price's criteria for architecture, as developed in the second edition of his *Essay*:

> ... the first principle in all architecture, whatever its style, must be the appearance, as well as the reality of firmness and stability; and whatever gives an idea of a false, or uncertain bearing, contradicts that first principle.... Natural objects are chiefly made up of different gradations of waving lines; and strait lines being rare, and proceeding more frequently from design than from accident, have in them an unnatural, or at least an artifical appearance. The reverse is true with respect to architecture: strait lines are in its very

essence; and any attempt to avoid them, must in general appear unnatural, or affected. Its curves also are regular and uniform...[12]

Price's clarity about the needs of his eye and their relation to what was manageable in reality was reflected in what he told Lady Beaumont some years later when she and Sir George were improving Coleorton: "The choice of the particular compositions from the principal windows, marks the difference between a person who has formed his taste on the principles of painting, and a mere lover of prospects.... When I built my small house at Aberystwyth, Lady Caroline and I consulted day after day about the exact position of the principal windows so that the composition might be precisely what we liked..." (26 June 1804)[13] While Castle House and its environs were obviously "interesting to the cultivated eye," it was at Foxley that this interest was combined with the practical excitement of "improving landscape" to the highest power of the picturesque.

III

Curiously enough, it is not Price in his roles as a visually sensible man or as a picturesque improver, or, as he would prefer, picturesque "painter"—we recall that in the first edition of the *Essay* he wrote that "when I speak of a painter, I do not mean merely a professor, but any man (artist or not) of a liberal mind, with a strong feeling for nature as well as art, who has been in the habit of comparing both together" (p. 9)— who emerges most strongly from the Coleor-

---

[12] *Essay*, 270–271.

[13] The house no longer exists; buildings of University College have incorporated its site. Nineteenth-century accounts of it may be read in several sources, among which are: *Topographical and Statistical Description of the Principality of Wales. II, South Wales* (London, n.d.), 128: "Contiguous to the ruins of the old fortress, Mr. Uvedale Price... has erected a fantastic house, in the castellated form... It consists of three octagon towers, with a balcony towards the sea. The rooms are well contrived, and elegantly furnished: the windows command an limited view of St. George's Channel, and the dilapidated walls of the castle, which are here viewed to great advantage..."; W. Bingley, *Excursions in North Wales* (London, 1839), 179; T. Roscoe, *Wanderings and Excursions in South Wales* (London, n.d.), 11: "A fantastic looking building, half gothic castle, half Italian villa, stands between the Church and the sea; it was built by the late Sir Uvedale Price, but is now used as a lodging-house..."; and T. Turner, *Narrative of a Journey* (London, 1840), 23: "Comparing it with the neighbouring fragments of the time-worn castle, what a strange mimicry of the antique does it evince."

ton Papers. Rather, it is Price the family man, a devoted and affectionate husband and father, who feels "so many consolations and pleasures at home" (28 January 1816), "and whose great pride in old age is that he is used to live *en famille*." (20 August 1823) So sustained was he by the health and stability of his personal relationship, that his energies were released to enhance what he was pleased to describe as "the beauty, connection, and comfort of my place." (24 July 1812)

Price's years at Foxley were spent "trying the effect of my own principles," he proudly informed Sir George (4 April 1804), and many came to Yazor in Herefordshire to see these results. Foxley was sought out by scores of distinguished persons who where pleased to come to enjoy Price's urbane conversation, to view his fine picture collection, and, in the words of a contemporary visitor, to find

> the labour of ascending his beautiful terrace, and of penetrating his luxurious wood...amply repaid, by a variety of...scenery....The house is finely situated...the grounds and plantations, which are very extensive, display the peculiar taste of the scientific proprietor and attract universal admiration. A charming ride, of nearly two miles in extent, through a wood of fine oaks, leads to the point of a hill called Lady Lift, where the view expands in a delightful manner. To the N-E it looks over Herefordshire, to the Clee-Hills in Shropshire, and the Malvern-Hills in Worcestershire; and, to the S-W, the famous St. Michael's Mount, in Monmouthsire, is a fine object, with the Hatteral-Hills, and the Brecon and Radnorshire mountains in the background.[14]

Another contemporary testified to "fine trees forming a kind of woody amphitheatre round the mansion...the distance being formed by various hills retiring in perspective...and the foreground by rich masses of wood...chiefly planted by the late Mr. Price [that is, Robert, Uvedale's father]; but the improvements made both in the woods and grounds by the present possessor, most eminently display his superior knowledge in the difficult science of landscape gardening."[15] Of Price's dedication to landscape gardening the Coleorton Papers are full; we must understand, however, that for Price the

---

[14] [George Nicholson] *The Cambrian Traverler's Guide*, 2d ed. (London, 1813), 642 and 645.
[15] *The Beauties of England and Wales*, VI (London, 1806), 581–582.

old-fashioned English garden, "or a small space near the mansion," really extends into the park to form an organic whole. He does admit in the first edition of the *Essay* that

> near the house picturesque beauty must, in many cases, be sacrificed to neatness; but it is a sacrifice, and should not wantonly be made. A gravel walk cannot have the playful variety of a bye road; there must be a border to the gravel, and that and the sweeps must, in great measure, be regular, and consequently formal: I am convinced, however, that many of the circumstances, which give variety and spirit to a wild spot, might be successfuly imitated in a dressed place; but it must be done by attending to the principles, not by copying the particulars. It is not necessary to model a gravel walk, or drive after a sheep track or a cart rut, though very useful hints may be taken from them both; and without having water-docks or thistles before one's door, their effect, in a painter's foreground, may be produced by plants that are considered as ornamental. I am equally persuaded that a dressed appearance might be given to one of these lanes, without destroying their peculiar and characteristic beauties.[16]

The history of Price and the picturesque landscape at Foxley is indeed one, according to the Coleorton Papers, of "attending to the principles," enhanced by a never-flagging enthusiasm for experimentation and exploration, which persisted well into Price's old age. At the age of seventy, after a combined attack of the indispositions referred to earlier, he informed Beaumont that "when it is a good day with me, I am thought to get a little into my old pace...but it is only for a spurt: if I go on a moment too long, or go too far afield I break down suddenly. As I have been caught more than once in that way, I am obliged to be tether'd; I hope, however, to get the rope longer and longer, and at last to slip clear away from it..." 22 August 1817) Price's qualities of resiliency and enthusiasm could be no more vividly presented than in the spectacle one summons in the mind's eye of the improver and the tether. At the age of seventy-two, fully recovered, he can tell Sir George that "I go on...highly interested and aroused; enjoying all myself...in pruning and clearing...and

---

[16] *Essay*, 1 and 26.

1. Jan Both, *Landscape*, William Hayes Ackland
Memorial Art Center, Chapel Hill, North Carolina
(photo: Ackland Memorial Art Center)

2. Anonymous, *Fantastic Landscape*, William Hayes Ackland
Memorial Art Center (photo: Ackland Memorial Art
Center)

3. Robert Adam, *Castle in a Landscape*, University of Glasgow (photo: University of Glasgow)

4. Sir Thomas Lawrence, *Sir Uvedale Price*, Boston, Museum
of Fine Arts (photo: courtesy, Museum of Fine Arts, Boston)

5. Iron Bridge at Coalbrookdale (photo: Ironbridge Gorge Museum Trust Limited)

6. Michael Angelo Rooker, *Iron Bridge at Coalbrookdale* Aberdeen Art Gallery, Schoolhill, Aberdeen
(photo: Studio Morgan)

7. William Payne, *A Country House in a Brownian Landscape*, William Hayes Ackland Memorial
Art Center (photo: Ackland Memorial Art Center)

8. François Boucher, *Landscape with a Mill and Ruins*, North Carolina Museum of Art, Raleigh
(photo: courtesy of North Carolina Museum of Art)

9. Anonymous, *East view of Castle House*, National Library of Wales, Aberystwyth (photo: National Library)

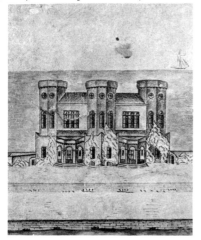

10. *East view of Castle House*, detail of
fig. 9

12. Anon., *Ruins of Aberystwyth Castle*,
det. Nat. Lib. of Wales, Aberystwyth
(photo: National Library of Wales)

11. *Aberystwyth Castle and Church*, coloured lithograph by Newman & Co.

13. Richard Wilson, *Snowdon*, Museum and Art Gallery, Nottingham
(photo: Castle Museum)

14. Paul Sandby, *Landscape with Bridge and Castle*, Dundee Art Museum, Dundee (photo: Dundee
Corporation)

15. Robert Price, *Picturesque Landscape with Trees*, Henry E. Huntington Art Gallery, San Marino (photo: Huntington Gallery)

16. Thomas Gainsborough, *Uvedale Tomkyns Price*, Bavarian State Painting Collection, Münich (photo: Bavarian State Collection)

17. Thomas Gainsborough, *Beech Trees in Wood at Foxley*, drawing, Whitworth Art Gallery, University of Manchester (photo: Manor Photographic Services)

18. Thomas Gainsborough, *La Forêt* after Jacob van Ruisdael Whitworth Art Gallery, University of Manchester (photo Manor Photographic Services)

19. Jacob Ruisdael, *Les Deux Paysans*, etching, Philadelphia Museum of Art (photo: Philadelphia Museum of Art)

shall probably go on making pictures and galleries [that is, composing his plantations according to picturesque principles] to the end of the chapter" (7 December 1818); in 1822 (12 November) he advises Sir George: "Here I have been, and here I am, much as you left me; ... upon the whole as active in mind and body as most men of 75: fond as I have always been of the place, I never took so lively an interest in it, never was so busy in forming extensive schemes of improvement.... I am now at work in a part you never saw, amidst such thickets and bowers of hollies mixed with yews and forest trees, such treasures of richness and intricacy that it would do your heart good to see them"; and at age seventy-seven, during one of his many visits to the properties of his arboricultural friends—in this case Lord Essex— he takes over, in the heat of the summer, describing his activities with enormous relish to Beaumont:

> In these two additional days I saw parts of the ground I had not seen before and some very fine trees particularly beech; ... I got to work on a very pretty spot called horseshoe dell, where cedars of Lebanon, red cedars, laurels, and many other exotics both evergreen and deciduous, had been planted some sixty or seventy years ago with great judgment or good luck on the top and sides of the surrounding banks, the *area* being left unplanted: this pretty spot had been long neglected, and quantities of seedling trees, chiefly ash had sprung up everywhere, filled up the whole area, and crowded, injured and concealed the fine old plants many of which, particularly some cock spur thorns had acquired remarkably wild picturesque forms. Lord Essex let me have some men, and we worked very hard tho' the weather was most sulky.... I was constantly on my legs to and fro in every direction... I cleared the area, cut down or framed whatever crowded or injured the old trees, made new communications and entrances into this little *sanctum*. I had not time to finish it, but begged Lord Essex not to let it be touched till I could in person renew my operations. (12 September 1824).

It is in this letter that Price uses a description of himself that shows clearly his basic freedom from the preciosity of picturesque chatter, and his realistic view of his primarily practical interests at Foxley, despite his considerable body of writings on the picturesque. "You," he tells Sir George, "are a professed generalizer," doubtless referring to Beaumont's somewhat contrivedly picturesque drawings and paintings. "I, tho' professedly picturesque, am very much of a tree-monger." Earlier on in the letters (4 August 1813)," he speaks of "my being so much used to the practical part and to deal with real trees, not with sham things of ink and chalk"; to Lady Beaumont a few years later (5 December 1817), he is deliciously sly when he comments to Lady Beaumont, "I rejoiced to hear that Sir George had taken the little pool in hand: I am not surprised, managing the pencil as he does, that he could prefer using it...to working with the spade, pick-axe &c...and yet, coarse instruments though they may be, you see what may be done by their aid when working under the eye of a painter, and guided by his so potent art. As he has got the outline to his mind, he must now set his palet: the improver's palet is his nursery..."

To be sure, a considerable part of Price's writings were devoted to arboriculture, and I believe the reason for this can be found in a passage in the first edition of the *Essay*, which demonstrates Price's deep involvement with the radical autonomy of visual criteria: "It is in the arrangement and management of trees that the great art of improvement consists: earth is too cumbrous and lumpish for man to contend much with.... But trees, detaching themselves at once from the surface, and rising boldly into the air, have a more lively and immediate effect on the eye. They alone form a canopy over us, and a varied frame to all other objects, which they admit, exclude, and group with, almost at the will of the improver...their beauty is compleat and perfect in itself, while that of almost every other object absolutely requires their assistance...it is perhaps from their possessing...variety and intricacy...in so eminent a degree, that trees are almost indispensably necessary to picturesque scenery." (pp. 206–209) As can be expected, there are many passages in the Coleorton Papers dealing with Price's tree compositions, but he evinces a curious ambivalence about these pursuits which can certainly be related to the tensions I referred to at the beginning,[17] the dialectic between accident and order, between emotion and principles.

[17] See above, p. 60.

To be sure, there is the straightforward account of picturesquing his trees: after confessing his uneasiness to Lady Beaumont regarding the hostilities between the British and the French, he wrote: "The only tactics I know, or even wish to know, is that of arranging and disposing trees, in larger or smaller bodies according to the nature of the ground.... Thinning and pruning with a proper mixture of caution and boldness is at least as necessary as planting...it is very pleasant to see single trees and groups rendered much more varied, light, and airy, by means of such clearing and pruning, which were before uniformly heavy and massy, for you will not suspect me of being an enemy to massivenes altogether, or of being likely to diminish the solemnity of my yews...." (August 1803) Yet, his "usual occupation of picture-making with the materials of nature" (10 January 1820) engenders a subtle feeling of guilt at perhaps tampering excessively with nature.

I know by experience how difficult it is to decide between a number of young and equally flourishing trees too close to one another; but you must be cruel to be kind: while they are in that state there is little room for choice, and anything is better than indecision: if you leave proper space between them, there will soon be a variety in their forms that will indicate motives.... It has been ingeniously said...that in every block of marble a fine statue is enclosed; you have only to clear away the rubbish: so it is with such a place as this; there are pictures in every tangled wood and thicket when the rubbish is removed: but what does, or does not constitute rubbish, is a very nice...point: you must not destroy the appearance of intricacy and wildness in the near parts, nor injure the mass and general outline from a distance, and must take special care, while you are clearing, to make one picture, not to sacrifice others in its neighbourhood: all this is to be considered before a stroke is struck.... This is particularly the case when I have discovered (and I am constantly on the look out) by peeping here and there through the boughs, and then going behind them, and looking again, that a certain portion of the distant hills, where the outline is most varied, might be happily introduced between trees

of a good form, if the middle trees, through which I had been peeping, and which might well be spared, were removed....
(5 December 1817)

Although elsewhere in his correspondence with the Beaumonts Price rationalized many of these activities by asserting that "nature has a great deal of execution, but very little taste," (10 January 1820) it is interesting to observe that in the last letter that he wrote to Lady Beaumont shortly before her death, he returned to the earlier theme: "I...know how much resolution it requires to cut down beautiful and flourishing trees, because they have flourished too much, and grown so as to mar the planter's intention: but on such occasions we must be cruel to be kind, or the trees will spoil one another; there will be no variety, no play of form or of outline, but a mere crowd of plants, a uniform mass of foliage." (19 August 1827)

The mansion at Foxley no longer exists, but some of the Price plantings do (Fig. 15). And if they did not, they have in a small but ineffaceable way been preserved for us by Thomas Gainsborough, who made music with the Price family, painted Uvedale's grandfather (Fig. 16), sketched with Uvedale's father, and travelled with Uvedale himself who worshipped him. One of Gainsborough's most poetical and resonant drawings is *Beach Trees in Wood at Foxley with Yazor Church in Distance* (Fig. 18). Done in brown chalk, watercolour and bodycolour over pencil, it is a *locus classicus* of Gainsborough's assimilation of the continental traditions of landscape painting (Figs. 18, 19) and his merging of it with his own ineluctable feeling for the picturesque motives, composition, and rendering which his young friend was to attempt to formalize. It is indeed a superbly wrought and elegantly realized composition of light, motion, intricacy, variety, and an asymmetry which irritates just to the point of stimulating. Just as the beech trees are the compositional center of the drawing, so was the tree itself for Price in his inventory to Lady Beaumont of trees "of great lightness and playfulness in their style of growing." (9 June 1804) "Playfulness"—a criterion not to be despised or dismissed: whatever the obsessive characteristics of the pursuit of the picturesque may have been, it still gave occasions for the self-realization of *homo ludens* and thus as a movement it transcends its quite respectable place in the history of landscape architecture to suggest provocative questions about complex human needs.

The English Garden in Hungary

ANNA ZÁDOR

The gardens discussed in this paper are later in time than those of similar style in Western Europe, for the history and development of Hungary, that small country in the eastern half of the continent, followed a different pattern. The hundred and fifty years of Turkish occupation, beginning toward the middle of the sixteenth century and ending at the end of the seventeenth century, destroyed a flourishing Late Gothic and a very formidable Cinquecento Renaissance of arts and architecture. It had spread from the court of King Mathias Corvinus, in the late fifteenth century, through the greater part of Hungary and had promoted the construction of fortifications and urban developments as well as the arts of sculpture and painting. Although the Turks did not intentionally devastate the vast areas of Hungary they held,[1] they naturally did not promote any further development of Hungarian art, nor did they do anything for the maintenance of existing buildings. The Turks built nothing except mosques, minarets and baths, features that give Hungary even today a very special character. Turkish occupation swept Hungary from the main stream of development; it was hard to rejoin it again.

It is clear that under such circumstances horticulture was relegated to the background,[2] survival and economic problems being more

[1] Hungary, a country of no more than 325,000 square miles, is surrounded almost entirely by high mountains, while the center of the country is occupied by the great Hungarian plain. The Turks held the central portion of Hungary. The non-occupied parts, that is the west and north regions and the eastern region called Transylvania, were on the whole independent of each other and belonged to different political and artistic spheres.

[2] On gardens in Hungary see: J. Bernouilli, *Reisen durch einen Teil des Königreichs Ungarn*, ed. G. Rothenstein (Vienna, 1763); *Die Gartenanlagen Österreich-Ungarns in Wort und Bild*

important, just as fortifications were far more important than the building of towns or mansions. On the other hand, this period of war and internal conflicts showed a marked predilection for and interest in botanical science. This is proved by the publication of a tripartite book on the garden of the bishop of Bratislava (Pressburg, Pozsony) by his brother, the Jesuit botanist János Lippai.[3]

The liberation of Buda took place in 1686. Hungary had suffered such disastrous damage that she had to start rebuilding almost from scratch. So the French Formal Garden with its costly programme did not have much chance in the first decades of the eighteenth century. However, the direct or indirect influence of the French court spread so rapidly over all Europe and also Hungary, that in the mid-eighteenth century Prince Nikolaus Esterházy built what can be called a Hungarian Versailles at Esterháza (now Fertöd) near the western border. It had a big and elaborate garden in the French style, with fine vistas and long stretches of artifical pools and ponds. The designer has not yet been established, but the lay-out may be due in part to the Prince himself, inspired not only by Versailles but also by Vienna.[4]

(Vienna, 1913); R. Rapaich, *Magyar kertek* [Gardens in Hungary] (Budapest, 1940). I. Ormos, *A kerttervezés története és gyakorlata* [History and Practice of Gardening] (Budapest, 1955). For the gardens mentioned on the following pages, see: J. Korabinsky, *Geographisch-historisches und Produkten Lexikon* (Pressburg, 1786); J. von Csaplovits, *Topographisch-statistisches Archiv des Königreichs Ungarn* (Vienna, 1821); M. Kunits, *Topographische Beschreibung des Königreichs Ungarn*, I–II (Budapest, 1824); J. A. Dorffinger, *Wegweiser für Fremde und Einheimische durch die Königliche Hauptstadt Pesth.* (Budapest, 1827); K. G. Windisch, *Geographie des Königreichs Ungarn* I–II (Pressburg, 1788); E. Fényes, *Magyarországnak és a hozzá kapcsolt tartományoknak mostani állapotja statisztikai és geográfiai tekintetben* [The Actual State of Hungary and its Annexed Provinces from a Geographical and Statistical Aspect], I–VI (Budapest, 1839); E. Fényes, *Magyarország geográfiai szótára* [A Geographical Dictionary of Hungary] (Budapest, 1851). A fundamental study based on the botanical aspects, but mentioning almost all the historical gardens of Hungary, was made by A. Pauer, *Adatok a magyar kerti kultura történetéhez* [Contributions to the History of Hungarian Horticulture] (Szombathely, 1926). For a general bibliography on the English Garden see M. Hadfield, *A History of British Gardening* (London, 1969), 441–446; D. Hennebo, A. Hoffmann, *Geschichte der deutschen Gartenkunst*, III (Hamburg, 1963), 295–303.

[3] J. Lippai, *Posoni Kert* [The Garden at Pozsony-Bratislava] (Vienna, 1664–67); A. Pigler, "A pozsonyi primási kert Szent György szobra" [The St. George Statue in the Garden at Pozsony] *Magyar Müvészet* [Hungarian Art], 1 (1925), 567, showing an engraving of the garden in the early eighteenth century. The importance of this Hungarian garden is stressed by M. Gothein, *Geschichte der Gartenkunst*, II (Jena, 1920), 255.

[4] *Beschreibung des hochfürstlichen Schlosses Eszterház im Königreich Ungarn* (Pressburg, 1784), with a plan and a series of engravings. Recently, the specialist on that garden, M. Möcsényi, published a series of papers: "A fertödi táj-park-kastélyegyüttesröl" [The Garden, Landscape and Mansion at Fertöd] in *Müemlékvédelem* [Historical Monuments], 10 (1966), 214–217; 11 (1967), 80–82, 228–234; 12 (1968), 171–176.

French gardens of smaller size with parterres and pools were built all over Hungary, except in the Great Plain but descriptions, original plans and travel books furnish little information about them. Indeed the French Formal Garden became a status symbol in the period between 1750 and 1770. The aristocracy of the imperial court as well as the Hungarian nobility were eager to boast of such gardens.[5]

We must understand the peculiarly slow development of Hungary and, in connection with this, the different way of adopting new ideas. In the late eighteenth century the influence of the French Encyclopedists and of French Rationalism was felt all over Europe. In Hungary, the Enlightenment was in great part coupled with Sentimentalism, especially in literature, as the main stream of influence in this respect came from Germany.[6] There was hardly a sign in Hungarian writing of what, in the West, was called the Age of Reason. The new ideas were spread by the upper classes, as the symbol of their links with the West, especially with the Vienna court.

The English Garden in its earliest examples also made its way into Hungary in this fashion. It did not involve a new civil and democratic development, in the sense of the Enlightenment, as it gained ground among the aristocracy only. Some promoters of the new garden type, however, were from the smaller gentry and the lower ranks of the clergy, mostly writers and priests. It was customary for a family of higher standing to have a priest or some other educated literary man living in their house as tutor to their sons, and to accompany them on their travels abroad. In the late eighteenth century, travelling, even if not as long and far as the usual English Grand Tour, came to be regarded as a source of knowledge and experience also in Hungary. In this way, members of the upper and the lower classes came into personal intellectual contact and became familiar with the mainstream of ideas and changes in taste in western Europe.

Not only the social conditions but also the geographical situation shaped the nature of landscape gardening in Hungary. The climate is hot in summer and cold in winter, with few rainy days. The English Garden with its vast lawns and numerous southern trees could be

---

[5] The French formal gardens are mentioned mainly in Korabinszky, *Lexikon*, Kunits, *Topographische Beschreibung*, and Csaplovits, *Topographisches Archiv*.

[6] See the very profound studies published by J. Szauder, *Az estve és az álom* [Night and Dream] (Budapest, 1970).

adopted only with difficulty in Hungary. Most of the gardens were situated in the western part of the country and around the capital. The financial aspect was also important. Naturally, gardens could only be afforded by the wealthy, since the care and maintenance of turf required considerable means. It was also essential that the owner should live on his estate, which was not usual before 1800, owing to the great attraction of Vienna. The highest rank aristocrats, the wealthiest owners lived there, perhaps even had an elegant *palazzo* in the city, and spent only a few summer weeks on their Hungarian estate.

I have no time to go into botany, but since one of the most important innovations of the English Garden was the use of unusual kinds of trees and shrubs, preserving their original shape and color, a few words have to be said about this aspect in Hungary. The years before and around 1800 were the most important ones for the development of Hungarian horticulture. A great variety of new species was introduced, and naturalization of various exotic plants took place. From that time on this trend developed steadily, reaching its peak in the second half of the century.

Preferred kinds of trees included the Lombardy poplar, the lime, the oak, the chestnut, various sorts of pines, the cypress, the acacia (locust) and the weeping willow, a very important feature of the English Garden. Bushes and shrubs of different origin, size and color complete the list, helped by importations from remote countries. The largest English garden of this period was Kismarton (Eisenstadt), where in the early nineteenth century Prince Paul Esterházy had more than 3,000 varieties of plants in his gardens and greenhouses, according to the detailed list drawn up by his chief gardener, Anton Niermeyer.[7]

Kismarton was not an isolated example, but from what is known of other notable gardens, they could not compare with its riches. It is possible, of course, that inventories have not come down to us. Lemons and oranges were grown in greenhouses, as well as numerous kinds of pelargonium, which latter has become a characteristic flower in Hungary. Knowledge of greenhouse construction was essential for

[7] A. Balogh, "Fertöd és Kismarton parkjai a XVIII és XIX század fordulóján" [The Gardens at Fertöd and Kismarton-Eisenstadt at the Turn of the Nineteenth Century], printed in *Kerteszeti és Szölészeti Föiskola Évkönyvei* [Annual of the Department for Gardening and Viniculture], (1953), 163.

the adaptation of exotic plants. It is almost certain that this knowledge came mainly from England, as was the case with Bernhard Petri as early as the 1780's.

In Germany, the English Garden style began in the second half of the eighteenth century and found an enthusiastic promoter in Goethe, whose prediliction for it may have been influenced by Hirschfeld's theories. The most famous English garden in Germany, Skell's at Schwetzingen, was inspired by English examples.[8] This is worth mentioning, as Germany had great influence on the development of the English Garden in Hungary.

It is rather difficult to fix a date for the introduction of the English Garden in Hungary, since the delayed development gave rise to a coexistence of the Formal and the English Garden. It seems that the English Garden appeared in Hungary later than in the west of Europe, hardly before about 1770. But no sooner was Esterháza, the "Hungarian Versailles", completed, than other trends in gardening and garden architecture emerged, as for instance at Csákvár, which was owned by the Counts Esterházy. We know about a series of gardens from descriptions in contemporary publications. Their owners were apparently proud of the new features and the spreading of knowledge of plants. After 1780, almost all formal gardens were transformed into English gardens, or at least had new parts added. The formal gardens were considered dull and impersonal. The accent on personality and individuality was a new feature, and it spread rapidly in Hungary.[9]

---

[8] Gothein, *Gartenkunst* II, 395.

[9] The following is a list of some formal gardens that acquired fame after being transformed into English ones; Acsád, Eördögh family estate, transformed in the last years of the eighteenth century, Pauer, *Hungarian Horticulture*, 12; Baloghfalva (Blhovce), where the formal garden surrounding the Koháry-Koburg mansion was transformed in 1803 into an English Garden, *ibid.* 29; Betlér (Betliar), not far from the latter, where the garden of the Nádasdy-Andrássy family was transformed into an English one around 1800, *ibid.*, 29. The Apponyi garden at Högyész had also been a formal garden decorated with sculpture and was transformed around the turn of the century into an English one, Fényes, *Dictionary*, II, 86. As far to the north as Homonna (Humenne) in Slovakia, we find a formal garden partly transformed into an English one (*ibid.*, 96), and mentioned again as a formal garden in the year 1861 in *Vasárnapi Ujság*, [Sunday Journal] 1861, 712–713. The famous Eszterházy mansion at Cseklész (Bernolakova), with its huge formal garden, mentioned in all the sources of the late 18th century (Korabinsky, *Lexikon*, 350–356, Windisch, *Geography of Hungary* I, 132), was transformed into a landscape garden after 1820, (Fényes, *Dictionary*, II, 20). Ivánka (Ivánka pri Dunasi) was treated in my paper on the garden plans in the Grassalkovich Archive, A. Zádor, "A. Grassalkovich levéltár kerttervei," found in *Magyar Müveszet* [Hungarian Art], 7 (1931), 595. This list also shows the diffusion of the Formal and later the English Garden all over Hungary, including Upper Hungary, now Slovakia.

From 1780 to the turn of the century a mixed garden style reigned that can be termed neither Rococo nor Picturesque. The garden widened into a landscape, open rather than restricted by structural or natural fences, and enriched by buildings in various styles. Turkish lodges, mosques and all sorts of other so-called "Turkish" garden architecture were the special feature in Hungary amid the exotic, the fantastic and the whole range of ornamental structures. Medieval architectural objects hardly appeared.

About 1800 attitudes changed. It was now almost impossible to lay out a garden, whether small or big, for the high nobility or for the smaller gentry, without incorporating some English features. As for the architectural structures considered so essential a few years earlier, hardly any were tolerated. No garden theatres, no fountains, no pergolas, only some statues were to be seen. The latter were common, for instance, in Transylvania. The open landscape, the hitherto unconsidered parts of nature, were now consciously merged into the English Garden, and soon became the main features. From then on into the middle of the nineteenth century the English Garden prevailed all over Hungary. Of course, in some remote places, and especially in smaller gardens owned by less up-to-date owners, the older taste survived. We have information about garden sculpture, as well as long vistas marked by a monument or an obelisk, but they do not represent the general trend.[10]

In the first decades of the nineteenth century an English garden was considered not only a symbol of up-to-dateness, but a sign of education. In his intimate and picturesque garden the man of western culture could stroll along the banks of sheets of water, amidst fine, often rare trees and shrubs, but few flowers. These features made the garden a world of its own, meant to be characteristic of its owner,

[10] Beside the gardens, decorated more or less richly with statues mentioned already or to be mentioned on the following pages, we have Pozsonynádas (Nádas Tristin), where the Motesiczky garden, even though an English garden, had garden sculpture (P. Jedlicska, *Kiskárpáti emlékek* [Memories from the Lower Karpats] (Pozsony, 1882), 18–90); Begaszentgyörgy (Begoj sveti Durad), estate of the Kiss family (Pauer, *Hungarian Horticulture*, 41); Högyész (Fényes, *Dictionary*, II, 212); Nagytétény near Budapest, a former Száraz-Rudnyánsky mansion with a series of garden sculptures (M. Aggházy, *A Barokk szobrászat Magyarországon* [Baroque Sculpture in Hungary], I (Budapest, 1959) 105); Nagyróna (Rovné), Erdödy mansion with sculpture in the garden, (Fényes, *Dictionary*, III, 301 and A. Mednyánsky, *Malerische Reise*, 130). The inventories of stone masons at Budapest (in course of publication by I. Dombi), have interesting information concerning garden sculpture for gardens near Budapest.

reflecting his sentiments and moods. This feature seems to have been
stressed by the Hungarian writer Kazinczy, a contemporary of Goethe
and an important advocate of Hungarian culture and poetry. He was
extremely fond of the English Garden style. His letters, dating from
the first years of the nineteenth century, also described the gardens
he saw in Slovakia and Transylvania, pointing out in great detail the
wealth of plants encountered and stressing the new style of the English
Garden.[11]

Now, who were the designers or architects of these first English
gardens? It is difficult to answer this question, as few plans have survived and signatures refer to largely unknown names.[12] Pattern books
with English garden designs must have reached Hungary at an early
date; the main publications from England, France or Germany were
mentioned as early as the late eighteenth century. Presumably, the
owners of the gardens had personal contacts with England, especially
the Protestant Hungarians of Transylvania. Occasionally, gardener
and architect worked together (as for instance at Kismarton), or the
plan of a garden was made by a surveyor and completed by the
gardener. The first person to be gardener as well as architect seems

[11] Ferenc Kazinczy (1759–1831) was a writer and leading figure in the Hungarian Enlightenment and a promoter of art. Besides theoretical and autobiographical writings, his main
works are his letters addressed to his friends, writers, poets and men of letters of Hungary,
published in twenty-two volumes with two complementary volumes and more to follow.
Kazinczy was aware of every new idea of his time, including the English Garden, whose
greatest promoter he was, although his main sources were German sentimentalism and his
approach in respect to artistic quality and taste was not always of the best. Yet he is one of
the main figures of this period. In his letters from the first years after 1800, he stresses the
beauty of the English Garden and the need for knowing its theory, "... valóban igen szükség
is, hogy tudgyák hazánkba mi legyen az Anglia kert, mi abból mind az izlés mind a me-
sterség. Hazánkbeli Anglus kertekbe többire csak a legdurvább irregularitásból áll azoknak
Anglussága, mint a cikornyás francia kertekbe." (It is essential that people in Hungary
should know what the English Garden means in taste and theory. It is supposed, here,
that it means only coarse irregularity, whereas an English Garden requires more rules and
care than the decorative Formal Garden). See, F. Kazinczy, *Levelezése, közzéteszi Váczy János*
[The Correspondence of F. Kazinczy, published by J. Váczy] IV (Budapest, 1893), 317.

[12] To mention some names, in addition to those that follow, we know of Bruning from
Dillenburg, who laid out the garden at Királyfalva (Krilova pri Senci, Slovakia), see Korabinszky, *Lexikon*, 324. George Bode designed the garden at Nagykároly (Carei, Roumania),
in 1793–1795, see Fényes, *Dictionary*, II, 181–182. In connection with the Orczy garden at
Budapest, Dorffinger, in the 1820's, speaks of Gregor Bene (Dorffinger, *Wegweiser durch Pesth*,
365), and as a specialist for garden architecture and fantastic buildings, we know about an
architect called Kinsky who spent the last years of the eighteenth century in Italy. See Becker's
Taschenbuch für Gartenfreunde, 1795. In Sárosd, the English garden surrounding the Esterházy
mansion is supposed to have been laid out by Eckler in 1819. See Kunits, *Topographische
Beschreibung* 94–95 and Fényes, *Dictionary*, IV, 14.

to have been Bernhard Petri (1768–1853), who spent four years in
England to learn the new style, and came to Hungary through Vienna.
He worked at Ráró and Vedröd (Voderady) in Slovakia, and also at
Hédervár in Hungary. Petri's English gardens became famous; he
gave an account and explanation of his own work in Becker's *Taschen-
buch für Gartenfreunde*.[13]

The garden at Hédervár, surrounding the Viczay mansion, was
transformed prior to 1786.[14] One of the first Englishmen to travel in
Hungary, Robert Townson, mentioned it as famous, saying that Viczay "had called the advice of a German who had resided a good
while in England with a view to learn the art of adjusting the scattered
careless beauties of rural scenery," which perfectly fits Petri.[15] It is
very probable that the main entrance to the mansion at Hédervár,
flanked by winged sphinxes, dates from Petri's period, although it is
perhaps not his own work, as he was neither sculptor nor builder.
Egyptian motifs, incidentally, are very rare in Hungary, and are
encountered mainly in that transitional period.

It was at Hédervár that Petri first tried his luck with the naturalization of the acacia, a tree which is still common in Hungary. But the
most important achievement of Petri is the laying out of the Orczy
garden at Pest, the first park in Hungary intended to provide open
space and fresh air to the inhabitants of a growing city. The density
of tree planting, as seen on a map dated 1810, had the purpose of
binding the sandy soil. This first public park was later mutilated, and
only a small part of it survives (Fig. 1).

Privacy was an essential characteristic of the English Garden. Tranquillity and solitude were indeed stressed, even in the plan. A city
park, on the contrary, is meant for a larger public, to offer it the benefit
of the style and features of the private garden. In this respect, the
Orczy park at Pest marks the beginning of a new period.

[13] On Bernhard Petri, see C. von Wurzbach, *Biographisches Lexikon des Kaisertums Österreich*,
XXII (Vienna, 1870), 110. Ráró was laid out in 1794, Vedröd some years later. Hédervár
is mentioned as being under construction in the 1780's, by M. Korabinsky, *Lexikon*, 228.

[14] See my paper on the garden plans of the Grassalkovich Archive mentioned in note 8
with earlier literature.

[15] R. Townson, *Travels in Hungary with a short account of Vienna in the year 1793* (London,
1797), 50; A. Vályi, *Magyarországnak leírása* [Description of Hungary] (Budapest, 1796), 86,
mentions the new garden in the English style, "az ángolj izléssel nem régen készült pompás
kert."

In Hungary, as in the United States, Greek Revival architecture was considered the national style.[16] There were, in fact, similar features of development in both countries. Greek Revival buildings were well suited for the English Garden style, and this fact enhanced by nationalism, is one of the factors explaining the fast spread of the English Garden in Hungary.

Another route of importation of the new gardening style very probably came from Lombardy. The Austrian occupation of Lombardy and the close ties between Austria and Hungary support this assumption. It is confirmed by the fact that Austrian architects worked in Milan. The outstanding figure among them was Leopoldo Pollach (Pollack), who in 1793 designed the sumptuous Villa Belgiojoso with its famous English garden. This garden figures as an important illustration in the first Italian work on English gardens, the one of 1803 by Count Silva. It showed the characteristic sinuous paths, a round temple and huge trees (Figs. 2, 3).[17] The brother of Leopoldo Pollach, Mihály Pollack, was the leading figure in Hungarian Greek Revival architecture, designer of a number of famous mansions with English gardens, to be discussed later. This being so, and Italy being, as is well known, one of the chief sources of inspiration for Hungarian Greek Revival architecture, is it not likely that his knowledge about the English Garden originated from his studies with his brother in Milan?[18]

To sum up, we may presume that the main sources of the English Garden in Hungary were pattern books and periodicals, such as Grohmann's *Ideenmagazin*, and also books on gardening and botany. Personal experience and contact with the new style in gardening also played an important part, as mentioned in connection with Petri. But the owners too had their wishes, making use of knowledge acquired abroad,

[16] A. J. Downing, *A Treatise on the Theory and Practice of Landscape Gardening adapted to North America* (New York-London, 1841).

[17] On the architect Pollack, see, A. Zádor, "Leopoldo Pollach és Pollack Mihály," *Archaeologiai Értesitö* [Archaeological Bulletin], 14 (1931), 189–244, and *idem*, "Leopoldo Pollach," *L'Arte*, n.s. 28 (1963), 3–41. A smaller garden by the same Austrian architect, the Villa Amalia in Erba-Incino, a center of the Italian Enlightenment, and the Villa Agliardi in Sombreno near Bergamo bear the same characteristic features. On the English Garden in Italy, see, N. Pevsner," Pedrocchino and some allied problems," in *Architectural Review*, 20 (1957), part 2, 113. R. Wittkower, "English Neo-Palladianism, the Landscape Garden, China and Enlightenment," *L'Arte*, ser. 3, vol. 6 (1969), 18–35.

[18] On Mihály Pollack, see my monograph, A. Zádor, *Pollack Mihály, 1773–1855* (Budapest, 1960).

as well as of the books and journals. Finally, geographically speaking, to England and Germany, Italy must be added as a source area.

I have called the first phase of the English Garden in Hungary a transitional phase. One of the most attractive examples of this period is the garden of the Counts Esterházy at Csákvár. A mansion built around 1781 by an unknown architect was transformed after 1800 into a large and impressive Greek Revival building, perhaps based on plans by Charles de Moreau and Engel. Very probably the English garden was laid out in the first building period, that is before 1800. It was richly decorated with a variety of architectural objects, such as a *Temple d'Apollon*, a *Gloriette chinoise*, a *Bâtiment turc*, and also a pyramid and a building in the Egyptian style. A recently discovered series of nine gouache paintings signed by a certain Peter Rivetti show views of the garden. The paintings are of poor quality, but they are of documentary interest. They show the sinuous paths and avenues of the English Garden, and weeping willows, poplars and oaks, and calm waters. But certain features of the Formal Garden, such as radiating avenues and garden theatres, are also still in existence. The gouaches date from 1783 to 1797, setting a date for the planning of the garden, but were not made before 1795, the first year that Rivetti is mentioned in the archives of the family. The fame of the garden at Csákvár, with its unusual richness of ornamental architecture, spread quickly, and it seems that the various rebuildings of the mansion did not alter this early English garden or its structures, some of which are still extant (Fig. 4).[19]

The same transitional style of the 1770's and 1780's appeared in various parts of Slovakia. Among these I want to mention Majorháza of the Jeszenák family, which Korabinsky described as early as 1796

[19] Who the architect of the garden and its building was, has not been established so far. The most detailed study about the gouaches was done by P. Kovács, "Beiträge zur Geschichte des Esterházy Parks von Csákvár im 18. Jahrhundert," in *Alba Regia, Annales Musei Stephani Regis, Székesfehérvár*, 10 (1969), 170–180, to whom I am also indebted for the photographs. Although this huge building and the park are mentioned many times, no definite facts are known. We hear about an earthquake in 1810, which ruined the building, and it is supposed that the mansion as it stands today was built after that. This would confirm the traditional attribution to Louis de Montoyer, active at Csákvár, as his plan for the rebuilding of the former Royal Palace at Buda is known from this year. See, *Hazai és Külföldi Tudósitások* [News from Home and Abroad], 1810, I, 92 and 1814, I, 323. Neither Charles de Moreau (1758–1844), nor Louis de Montoyer (1749–1811) have so far been treated in depth, although they are important for the architecture of Austria. See, R. Wagner-Rieger, *Wiens Architektur im 19. Jahrhundert* (Vienna, 1970), 40, n. 56; 42, nn. 76–77. On Engel, who worked presumably also at Csakvár, a study (by I. Bibó) with surprising plans is just published.

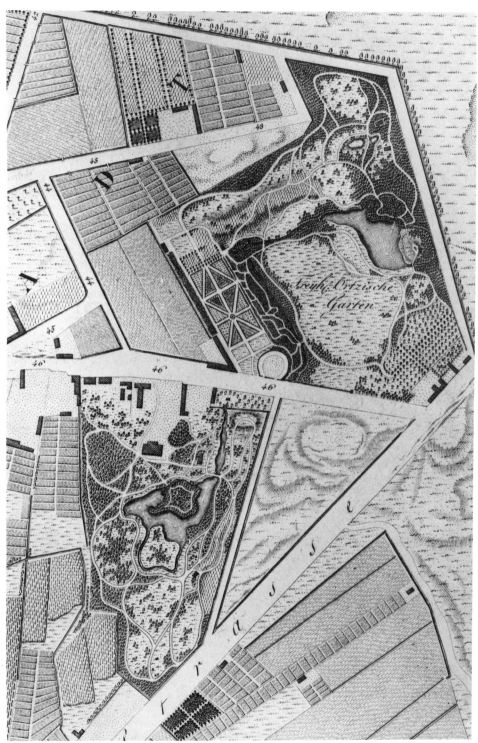

1. Orczy Garden, Pest, detail of the map made by J. Lipszky in 1810 (Historical Museum of Budapest, no. 14.755–2)

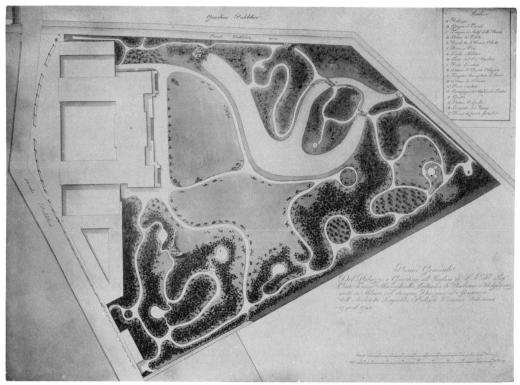

2. L. Pollach, plan of the English garden of the Villa Belgioioso at Milan, 1793 (formerly in the Archivio di Stato, Milan)

3. L. Pollach, Villa Belgioioso, engraving from Silva, *Dell'Arte dei Giardini Inglesi*

4. Pyramid and *Maison Egyptienne* at Csákvár, gouache
by P. Rivetti (photo: K. Kónya)

5. Decorations at Hotkóc (Hodkovce), detail from J. Rombauer
(photo: J. Karáth)

6. Decorations at Hotkóc (Hodkovce), detail from J. Rombauer
(photo: J. Karáth)

7. In the garden at Tata (photo: J. Rados)

8. Charles de Moreau, Artificial Ruin in the garden of Tata (photo: J. Rados)

9. Charles de Moreau, the Turkish House at Tata (photo: J. Rados)

10. The *Monopteros* at Kismarton (photo: J. Rados)

11. Garden and *tempietto* at Kismarton, painting by J. Fischer (OL, former Eszterházy Archive, vol. 42, no. 1379)

12. Mansion and garden at Gernyeszeg-Gernesti, lithograph by Rohbock (published in the volume, *Hungary and Transylvania*, 1857)

13. View of the English garden at Körmend (Photo Collection of the Center for Preservation of Historical Monuments, no. 8.737)

14. The former Festetich villa and garden at Budapest, lithograph by Barth (Historical Museum of Budapest, no. 188.14)

15. A view in the garden at Dég (Photo Collection of the Center for Preservation of Historical Monuments, no. 48.683)

16. Mansion and garden at Fót, painting by K. Klette, 1835 (Budapest, Portrait Gallery of the
Hungarian National Museum, no. T. 5530, photo: J. Karáth)

17. In the garden at Martonvásár (Photo: K. Örsi)

18. The former Brunswick mansion at Alsó-Korompa, Dolny Krupa (Photo Collection of the Museum of Architecture, Budapest, photo: T. Mihalik)

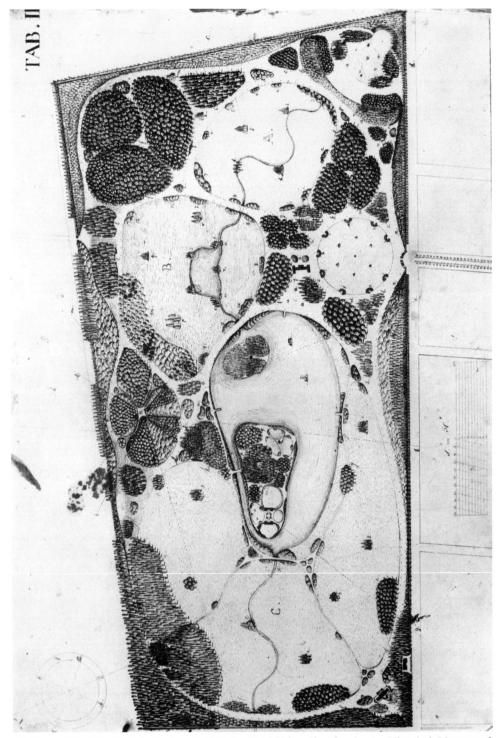

19. Plan of the City Park in Budapest, 1816 by H. Nebbien (drawing in the Historical Museum of Budapest, no. 66.165.1)

20. Design for the entrance building of the City Park in Budapest by H. Nebbien

21. Lake with island in the City Park in Budapest, lithograph by R. Alt and F. J. Sandmann (Historical Museum
of Budapest, no. 3317/12)

22. Mansion and garden at Nagyugróc (Velké Uherce), lithograph by J. Zürnich (Portrait Gallery of the Hungarian National Museum, no. T. 6017)

23. Mansion and garden at Sárospatak, lithograph by G. Kelety.

as a new attraction with a Gothic House and a Turkish Tomb.[20] The most sophisticated of the transitional gardens may have been Hotkóc (Hodkovce), described in detail by Kazinczy. There is a painting by Johann Rombauer (1782–1849) dated 1803, containing twenty-three views of the Hotkóc garden. The owner, Count Emmanuel Csáky was apparently so proud of having created this garden, that he commissioned its portrayal instead of his own portrait. It was he who invited Kazinczy to visit, and to that we owe the detailed description published in 1806. The mansion itself, transformed from an old barn, is not very ambitious. The entrance gate and some other architectural structures display shapes and style of the late Baroque, whereas the *Tempietto*, a Gothic church, and some statues have both medieval and neo-classical connotations. The plan of the whole garden is not known, but it must have been similar in style to *Anglo-chinois* gardens of western Europe. Kazinczy, who seems to have been aware of the importance of this new trend, made reference to Hirschfeld and Grohmann, both popular in these years. Kazinczy adds pointedly that while everybody feels he must possess an English garden, few care enough to learn its art and theory properly (Figs. 5, 6).[21]

In the description of Hotkóc, Kazinczy refers to the large and famous English garden of Tata near Csákvár, owned likewise by the Esterházy family. The English gardens of both Csákvár and Tata can be discerned on the maps of 1784, made for the whole of Hungary on the orders of Joseph II,; so we may safely assign a very early date to both. It seems that they were begun, if not finished, simultaneously.[22] We have at Tata two gardens, both with attractive stretches of water, which add to their feeling of calm and spaciousness. Some parts of the old castle, its bastions and fortifications, were still extant, and they were included in the new plan, adding a romantic feature to the layout of the vast garden (Fig. 7). Another important feature of the garden at Tata is the artificial ruin built around 1801 by Charles de Moreau,

[20] For Majorháza see Korabinsky, *Lexikon*, 394–395.

[21] F. Kazinczy, "Hotkóc, Anglus kertek" [English Gardens], in *Hazai Tudósitások* [News from Hungary], 1816, 262–263; 268–271; 276–280, and idem, *Correspondence*, IV, 316–328. The Rombauer picture (54 × 81.5 cm) is in the Department of Historical Portraits of the Hungarian National Museum, no. 2086. It was first mentioned in a lecture given by Mrs. Éva Szentléleky-Koroknay in the 1950's.

[22] As a follower of Kazinczy stressing the importance of theoretical knowledge, a study by F. Szeder may be mentioned, "Az Anglus kertekről" [On English Gardens] in *Tudományos Gyüjtemény* [Scientific Papers], 1 (1825), 76–103.

an important architect of the early years of the nineteenth century.
He incorporated fragments of Roman and medieval buildings brought
to light in the neighborhood, especially large numbers of beautifully
carved architectural details from the former Benedictine abbey church
at Vértesszentkereszt. Moreau's ruin is set on a sloping part of the
garden with a stream whose bed was channelled for this building.
The ruin has an aisled nave and no roof. With its surroundings, it
makes a sentimental contrast with the rich growth of the garden. The
mixture of the picturesque with the sentimental reflects the ideas of
Rousseau, which were spreading fast among the aristocracy in Hungary.
The connection between Tata and Csákvár is stressed also by a small
Turkish pavilion, perhaps less naïve than the one at Csákvár. Neither
of these pavilions has anything in common with those more Baroque
structures in German gardens which are called Turkish. Although
Moreau came from Vienna, the ruin he designed does not resemble the
one at Schönbrunn composed mainly of ancient fragments (Figs. 8, 9).[23]

Besides the ruin at Tata, only the mansion and park at Kismarton
can be attributed to Charles de Moreau. The original castle was
rebuilt several times, then remodelled into a château and surrounded
with a formal garden in the early eighteenth century from the designs
of Louis Gervaia. The garden was too old-fashioned for Prince Paul
Esterházy, a collector of paintings and a man of high views as to his
importance. In the last years of the eighteenth century he began to
enlarge his mansion and added a vast English garden with that wide
variety of plants mentioned earlier in connection with Niermeyer's
botanical lists.[24] We have evidence that Moreau worked from 1801
on the lay-out of the garden, which he considered overcrowded with
tall trees but lacking in enclosed and intimate spots. Moreau had a
team of engineers and other specialists, mainly trained in England, at
his disposal to carry out the modifications. The general lay-out of the

[23] As for Tata it is again Kazinczy who mentions it for the first time. *F. Kazinczy, Ferenc
utja Pannonhalmára, Esztergomba, Vácra* [Travels to Pannonhalma, Esztergom, Vác] (Budapest,
1831). The ingenious waterworks and engineering at Tata are due, perhaps to the great
hydraulic engineer of the 18th century, Samuel Mikoviny, who worked at Tata as early as
1727 and 1748. Korabinsky, *Lexikon*, 126; Townson, *Travels in Hungary*, 52; J. Rados, *Tata*
(Budapest, 1954); A. Zádor, "Zur Frage der französischen Revolutionsarchitektur in Ungarn,"
Actes du XXIIe Congrés internationale d'histoire de l'art, Budapest, 1969 (Budapest, 1972), now
in press. On Rousseau in this connection, see E. M. Neumeyer, "The Landscape Garden as
Symbol in Rousseau, Goethe, Flaubert," *Journal of the History of Ideas*, 8 (1947), 187–217.
[24] See above, p. 82.

garden has survived until today, very much in its original shape, but the condition has deteriorated. It was enriched by a big canal, four artificial lakes and numerous paths, showing a great variety of design. The park has various levels and is framed by hills and mountains that turn it into real landscape. On one of the most exposed eminences is a *monopteros*, dedicated to the Prince's sister Leopoldina, whose statue by Canova is inside. The temple is very similar to those at Wörlitz and the *Englische Garten* in Munich, but its situation is more attractive. Facing the lake and surrounded by its richly varied trees, it is a very picturesque sight with its air of placidity (Fig. 10). Kismarton had heatable greenhouses, among the earliest in this part of Europe. The great complex marks the end of the period of transition. The picture-like aspect of the garden, so characteristic of this early time, may be seen in a painting by the Viennese Josef Fischer (1769–1822), the court painter to the prince and director of his picture gallery. Fischer condensed in one small picture all the features of the garden and rendered its original look remarkably well (Fig. 11).[25]

In the first decades after 1800, the English Garden became more and more a symbol of the social status of the owner; formal gardens rapidly disappeared and the mythological statues in favour in the late Baroque and in the early phase of the Greek Revival now rarely occurred in these gardens. Nevertheless, some are found in Transylvania. For instance, at Kerlés (Chirales) Count Lajos Bethlen built a mansion around 1810–1813 and adorned his small English garden with mythological statues by the Viennese sculptor Schmutzer. Kazinczy, who saw Kerlés in 1816, was impressed. The plan for the garden may have originated in Vienna, and there must originally also have been some architectural structures.

There were also statues at Gernyeszeg (Gernešti), an estate with an impressive Late Baroque mansion and a garden with large areas of

---

[25] Whether we are justified in considering the engineer of the prince, a certain Jakob Rauschenfels, who signed the plan, as the designer of the whole garden under the guidance of Moreau, is not yet decided. The plan and elevation for the greenhouse bears his signature, with the caption: "Plan des Ganzen zur Treiberey gehörigen Terrains im Eisenstaedter Hofgarten," Eszterhazy Papers, 44, no. 1510, Országos Levéltár, TEGY [State Archive of Hungary]. On Kismarton-Eisenstadt, see Csaplovits, *Topographisches Archiv*, II, 144: D. Frey, *Die Denkmäler des politischen Bezirkes Eisenstadt und der Freien Städte Eisenstadt und Rust* (Vienna, 1932), 55; J. Rados, *Magyar kastélyok* [Hungarian Castles] (Budapest, 1943), 21–215; A. Valkó, "Moreau a kismartoni diszkert rendezéséröl," [Moreau on the Remodelling of the Garden at Kismarton-Eisenstadt], in *Annales Horti et Viniculturae*, vol. 28, Tom. II, fasc. 1, p. 101.

apparently boundaryless water surrounded by the typical trees of the period (Fig. 12). Around a pool built on the site of the former moat were satirical statues of Mirabeau, Louis XVI and other personalities of the French Revolution represented as dwarfs. They seem to belong to an earlier phase of the building; it is not impossible that they were imported from another mansion.[26] They show the important role assigned to sculptural decoration in gardens, even in remote districts. Gernyeszeg, for instance, had pavilions, obelisks and other garden architecture, as may be seen in a plan signed by two Hungarian engineers and dating from 1831, but showing a later lay-out.

The gardens in the mountainous countryside of Transylvania were not as large as those on level ground in other parts of Hungary. The variety of levels, however, added impressive contrasts, heightened by rich vegetation and rivers as well as canals. As the owners generally lived on their estates, Transylvanian gardens had an air of distinct individuality. They were neither as elegant nor as richly decorated as the gardens already mentioned. They tended to be somewhat mixed in style and conservative, retaining features of earlier style gardens, but all this added individuality and at the same time pleasing dignity.

It is to be noted that in the first quarter of the nineteenth century this mixed style in garden architecture, conserving some Late Baroque features in sculpture, can be found in other parts of the country as well. In the same years of the nineteenth century an attractive example of an English garden is found for instance in north Hungary, at Szécsény, surrounding the former Pulszky mansion. The most attractive parts of this composition by an unknown garden architect are placed around a lake-like stream surrounded by trees, shrubs and flowers. The remoteness and quiet of the garden fits well into the mood of the time. Fényes refers to Szécsény as an elegant English garden, but no hint as to its designer has been found so far.[27]

In the former Batthyányi garden at Körmend, begun after 1795 and completed before 1820, the large lawn was between winding paths

[26] On Kerlés (Kerles), see F. Kazinczy, Erdélyi levelek (Letters from Transylvania), ed. G. Kristóf, I (Kolozsvár, 1944), 77; L. Bethlen, Onéletirása [Autobiography by L. Bethlen] ed. L. Szádecky (Kolozsvár, 1909), 30. On Gernyeszeg (Gernesti), see J. Biró, A gernyeszegi Teleki Kastély [The Teleki Mansion at Gernyeszeg] (Budapest, 1934), 34; idem, Erdélyi Kastély-ok [Mansions of Transylvania] (Budapest, 1943), 6–114.

[27] On Szécsény, see Fényes, Dictionary, IV, 74.

enclosed by a wall of trees. It has a *point de vue* and an obelisk.[28] The garden was presumably laid out by the garden architect Carl Wessely, the Flora and Pomona groups were by the Viennese sculptor. J. M. Fischer. In a letter dated 2 February 1807, Kazinczy mentions the garden, proving the assumption that it belonged to the early examples transformed from a formal garden prior to 1780 (Fig. 13).

An obelisk is mentioned in a smaller garden in Slovakia at Csuz (Čuz) belonging to the Csuzy family. It has grottoes and small transportable bridges, a hermit's cave without a hermit, richly furnished greenhouses with exotic plants, and fine rare trees all over the estate. The whole is a remarkable example of old and new, with an intimation of the romantic and sentimental (Fig. 14).

I have already drawn attention to early English gardens in Hungary influenced by Italy.[29] We have only to remember the designs by L. Pollach and compare then with the Festetich garden in Pest, whose small "villa" was built prior to 1803 by Michael Pollack. The "villa" was surrounded by one of the earliest English gardens in Pest, later transformed into a botanical garden. The original plan, on the map by Lipszky, shows its lay-out clearly. On the other hand, a small part carved out of the already mentioned Orczy garden was merged by Pollack into the gardens of the Military Academy (Ludoviceum) built in the 1830's.[30] A contemporary engraving conveys the sense of space and remoteness, and the nostalgia for tranquillity and solitude. Here we have no more decorative fantastic buildings, no more embellishments. Pollack's gardens are not picturesque but sentimental. The effect is entirely that of real landscape. The most famous of his gardens was at Alcsut near Budapest, made for the Hungarian Palatine Duke Joseph Hapsburg around 1820. It was almost completely destroyed during the Second World War. Instead of Alcsut we may look at the former Festetich estate at Dég, built by Pollack in the early 1820's. It was a center of freemasonry. Dég has a monotonous flat site, but the garden transformed it into an attractive landscape. The big lawns and carefully chosen and placed trees enhance the

[28] See, Kunits, *Topographische Beschreibung*, I, 144. A letter written by Kazinczy mentions a monument in honor of Gessner (dated 2 February, 1807) in *Correspondence*, IV, 423. Rapaich, *Gardens in Hungary*, 200. All this increases the possibility of the garden having been laid out around 1780.

[29] See above, p. 87.

[30] E. Fényes, *Present State of Hungary*, I, 15.

effect of the very elegant building, and the part with the lake-like rivers and Dutch House looks like a painting (Fig. 15).[31]

Similar features are found in the garden of the Károlyi mansion at Fót, built by an unknown architect in the days of Pollack. The original plan for the garden, perhaps made in the 1820's by the garden architect Ignác Erményi, has not survived. But two pictures, one signed and dated 1835, by a minor painter, Károly Klette, present a full view of this very typical Hungarian garden with its large expanses of lawn, groups of shrubs, and clumps of not too high trees, and an artifical lake in which swans used to swim majestically. The whole complex is on the border of the great Hungarian plain, framed to the north by hills of varied shape and height. All this, once again, creates a feeling of seclusion and serenity (Fig. 16).[32]

In the first quarter of the nineteenth century, almost every garden was made English. We know of a number of such gardens although there are no surviving plans or other documentary evidence. A fine example is at Lovasberény, the estate of the Cziráky family; another is the very elegant garden at Oroszvár (Carlsburg), traditionally connected with Moreau and laid out in the first years of the century. A journal of 1802 mentions that the Emperor and his court fled to this house with its recently redesigned garden during the Napoleonic Wars.[33] It was considerably transformed in the 1830's.

This series of large gardens ends with the famous Martonvásár estate of the Brunswicks, friends and patrons of Beethoven. Today this mansion contains a small Beethoven museum. It is not yet established whether Beethoven's *unsterbliche Geliebte* may be identified with the Countess Theresa Brunswick. Anyway Beethoven liked to stay at the house and stroll in the garden. Originally the estate covered about fifty-five square miles, surrounding the Baroque mansion. Theresa Brunswick refers in her diary to the rondel enclosed by lime trees,

[31] The original plans for Alcsut, Dég, and also Szöny, a smaller estate with a carefully laid out English garden done by Pollack, were destroyed during the Second World War. On Pollack see my monograph, *Pollack Mihály*.

[32] L. Grof Károlyi, *A nagykárolyi Károlyi család összes jószágainak birtoklási története* [A History of the Possessions of the Károlyi Family], I (Budapest, 1911), 67–68: V. Bierbauer, "A magyar klasszicizmus kastélyai" [Neo-classic Mansions in Hungary], *Magyar Müvészet* [Hungarian Art], 3 (1927), 224–234; J. Rados, *Magyar kastélyok* [Hungarian Mansions] (Budapest, 1943), 229; E. Révhelyi, "Az egyetemutcai volt Károlyi palota épitésének története" [History of the Building of the Károlyi Palace at Budapest], *Tanulmányok Budapest multjából*, [Studies on the History of Budapest], 2 (1933), 39–40.

[33] See, *Magyar Hirmondó* [Hungarian News], 1 (1802), 745.

and to the spacious lawns and big lakes surrounded by weeping willows (Fig. 17).[34] A lithograph dating from the middle of the nineteenth century displays the same features, and it seems that the garden was not altered even when, in the second half of the nineteenth century, the mansion was remodelled in the neo-Gothic taste, as it stands today. The characteristic features of the English garden with fine trees carefully set around water have persisted, adding a further attraction to this important cultural center. We do not know the name of the designer, but he might have been that of another Brunswick estate, the one at Alsó-Korompa (Dolny Krupa), in Slovakia, a certain Henry Nebbien. We are told that he transformed the formal garden of Alsó-Korompa into an English garden before 1817 (Fig. 18).[35]

The main features of this garden—high trees and shrubs around a Greek Revival building, and a large lawn divided in two by a stream—were at this time also common in Hungary and Slovakia. Another example is Vysny Blh, built around 1817–1822.

Henry Nebbien, the designer of Alsó-Korompa, worked in Budapest, where he was the architect of the large city park called Városliget. He won the competition for this in 1817. We know that he was French or Belgian by origin and that his garden designs were English. The park he created is similar to all other city parks laid out in the early 1800's. Nebbien accompanied his designs for this park with a detailed description of the history and aims of such parks, specifying all the trees, shrubs and flowers he intended to plant. We learn from this document that it was Nebbien who took the first steps in landscape gardening for the Brunswicks at Alsó-Korompa. It is quite possible that Martonvásár also is in some way connected with Alsó-Korompa and Pest. According to Nebbien, the pioneer of gardening was William Kent, and he believed that Kent had made England the leading country in garden design. But the most important feature in the eyes of Nebbien, the conveying of a sense of the infinite, does not belong

---

[34] On Martonvásár, see A. Balogh, "A martonvásári kastély és parkja" [The Mansion and Garden at Martonvásár], *Müemlékvédelem*, 10 (1966), 210–213. On Theresa Brunswick, see M. Czeke, H. Révész, *Grof Brunswick Teréz* [Countess Theresa Brunswick] (Budapest, 1926). On Alsókorompa (Dolny Krupa), see, P. Jedlicska, *Kiskárpáti emlékek* [Memories of the Low Karpats], II (Budapest, 1882), 151, calling Nebbien a gardener of Belgian origin. Fényes, *Dictionary*, I, 249. A Zádor, J. Rados, *A klasszicizmus épitészete Magyarországon* [Neo-classical Architecture in Hungary] (Budapest, 1943), 196.

[35] I. Kuhn, *Klassicisticka Architektura na Slovensku* (Bratislava, 1955), fig. 106. Nebbien writes in his petition for the park of Pest (1817) that he had just finished his work at Alsókorompa.

to Kent but to Repton. The landscape garden is no longer the echo of landscape painting, it is nature remodelled for eternity.

Nebbien included in his manuscript for Városliget thirteen drawings and water-colors, in one of which we can see a big lake with two islands and a small bridge (Fig. 19). Spacious lawns with clumps of trees and shrubs were laid out in an irregular manner. There were also some smaller buildings, a ballroom pavilion, a restaurant, etc. But the feature most characteristic of Nebbien's work is the imposing and almost over-sized main gate, a semicircular colonnade, topped by a piece of triumphal sculpture. It is as grandiose as the entrance to an imperial residence. However, it is a very retardataire idea for these years, reminiscent of French architecture before and under Napoleon. In any case, this curious and ambitious structure was, for financial reasons, never built. The city park soon became a popular spot for picnics, and remained unaltered for many decades, as the subtle and sentimental lithographs by Rohbock and Rudolf Alt show (Figs. 20, 21).[36]

The city park in Budapest is important for the spreading of the garden style in Hungary and especially in Budapest, which became the capital of Hungary in the early nineteenth century. We do not know whether Nebbien, who received approbation for his plan for Városliget from the Palatine Duke József, was also responsible for the design of that duke's huge private garden on Saint Margaret Island on the Danube in Budapest. A map dated 1811, showing an earlier phase of the island, displays the usual characteristics of a landscape garden. Later it must have been transformed into a more elaborate and articulated one, better suited to such a vast area. A water-color by Franz Jaschke (1775–1842) from the late 1830's (with the Summer Palace of the Palatine) shows all the well-known features of an English garden on a large scale.[37] The serenity and spaciousness of the island,

[36] For Nebbien's competition work see, "Ungarns Volksgarten der Königlichen Frei Stadt Pesth, 1816," (no. E. T. 66. 165), Historical Museum of Budapest, Department at Kiscell. Dr. I Bibó was kind enough to draw my attention to another competition design by Nebbien, this one of 1820, for the entrance gate of the Royal Palace at Vienna, Coll. Architekturzeichnungen, Mappe 66, Umschlag 6, nn. 30–36, Albertina, Vienna. The lithographs by Alt and Sandmann are also in the collection at Kiscell, no. 3, 316/12 and no. 549/17 (lithographs by Rohbock). On the city park see, T. Thaly, *A 200 éves Városliget* [The 200th Anniversary of the City Park] (Budapest, 1956).

[37] Details from the "Ökonomische Aufnahme von der Gegend bei Pesth im Jahr 1811, aufgenommen und gezeichnet von Josef Eggendorfer unter der Direktion des Herrn Frantz

and the enormous trees compensate for the monotony of the level ground. The sentimental character is enhanced by the wide arms of the river hugging it. This kind of garden, private but open to the public at certain hours, was not uncommon during the former Hapsburg monarchy. A little known example is a very picturesque garden near Zagreb, now in Jugoslavia, whose owner, a bishop of Zagreb, was of Hungarian origin. He apparently was proud of having produced such a beautiful garden, and indeed it may well have been unique in Croatia. The bishop invited a lithographer named Johann Zaschke to Zagreb in 1850 to make drawings of the garden. These the owner published as lithographs in an album accompanied by a description. The garden is of great extent, with fine trees, and it features various smaller architectural structures.[38]

City parks and the like contained, in general, no important buildings even when mansions or other smaller structures were erected. In private gardens, on the other hand, when a mansion formed the nucleus, it is remarkable how slight the connection between house and garden was. The need was never really consciously felt in Hungary in this period; on the contrary, the mansions were more or less hidden, and only in the earliest gardens could one have the feeling that some building was the center of some part of the garden. Generally there was a level terrace or lawn in front of the main building, and trees formed a frame around it, but otherwise architecture and garden were considered separate elements. They did not merge into an architectural complex in the way they had done in formal gardens. Hence, English gardens could be attached to any type of mansion. Most of them accompanied Greek Revival buildings, a style which goes well in composition and taste with English gardens, but neo-Gothic buildings, new or remodelled, were also often accompanied by gardens of this style. Beside Martonvásár, which I have already discussed, I can point to a mansion in upper northern Hungary, Nagy Ugróc (Velké Uherce, Slovakia) where the building as well as the garden seem to be an

---

Simm Ingenieur," (5.164, Historical Museum in Budapest). The water color by Jaschke is in the same collection, no. 15.674. For the Island and its pictorial representations see, D. Rexa, *Margitsziget* [Margaret Island] (Budapest, 1940).

[38] [J. Zaschke], *Park Jurjavés* (Vienna, 1852–53), Album no. 1826–63, Collection of Historical Portraits, Hungarian National Museum. I am indebted to Mrs. G. Wilhelmb-Czenner for having mentioned this rare publication to me, which later I found in the Garden Library at Dumbarton Oaks.

illustration taken from a pattern book (Fig. 22). Only the low height
of the trees and the predominance of exposed pines remind us of its
northern situation.[39] The same comment can be made about the
Transylvanian estate of the Bánffy at Bonchida (Bontida), which had
been in the possession of this prominent family for several centuries.
The late medieval castle was rebuilt repeatedly and finally was transformed into a mansion with a formal garden, often called the Transylvanian Versailles. Around 1830 an English garden was laid out,
designed by two engineers of Kolozsvár (Cluj). This garden remained
unaltered even when the central part of the mansion received its neo-
Gothic form. Bonchida may well be the first neo-Gothic building in
Transylvania. The English garden survived and offered picturesque
views along sinuous paths on the winding banks of the Szamos.[40]

At Bonchida the central part of the building dates from the late
Middle Ages, and the same is true of Sárospatak in the easternmost
part of Hungary. It has a keep with added Renaissance decoration
and a central range in the romantic style. The house was built for
the Bretzenheim family in the middle of the nineteenth century. The vast
English garden, partly on the site of the former moat, is planted with
oaks and chestnut trees, very characteristic of Hungary. (Fig. 23).[41]

The popularity of the English Garden in Hungary is proved by the
fact that printed sources, although rather scarce, furnish data on
almost two hundred of them. The tradition continued until the middle
of the nineteenth century. Those which survived the Second World
War, without or with only slight alterations, are partly under reconstruction and preservation, a process greatly helped by the Inter-
national Federation of Landscape Architects session of UNESCO,
which stressed the importance of gardens as historical monuments.[42]

[39] A lithograph by Josef Zürnich in the Historical Portrait Collection of the Hungarian
National Museum, no. 6.017. I am indebted to the architect Dr. L. Vargha for having mentioned it to me.

[40] Originally it had an area of almost 300 hectares, but the English garden did not occupy
the whole estate. Among the numerous architectural structures there was a *tempietto* and a
Solitude which already displays neo-Gothic motifs. See, J. Biró, *A bonchidai kastély* [The Mansion at Bonchida] (Cluj, 1935), 32–34 and *idem, Mansions in Transylvania*, 81.

[41] On Sárospatak there is a vast modern literature, but hardly anything concerning the
garden.

[42] Following the resolutions of the Icomos and IFLA Symposia (September 13–17, 1971),
held at Fontainebleau, about Hungarian gardens and their actual state from the points of
view of preservation of historical monuments, a basic paper by K. Örsi, "Az elmult lo év
kertépitési eredményei a müemlékirodalomban" [The Results of the Preservation of Historical
Gardens in the Last Ten Years] was published in *Müem lékvédelem* 15 (1971), 129–1247.

The Arrival of the
English Landscape Garden
in Poland and Bohemia

The arrival of the English Garden in Po-
land is by now well documented. It coincided with what, although
it included the disaster of the Partitions, for the Poles is one of the
more heartening phases of their history—the national rebirth of *Oświe-
cienie*, the Enlightenment. In architecture, this movement's most characteristic product is not the columned town palace or the domed
cylindrical church, but the country house with its park. And its park
is the Landscape Garden which the Enlightened gentleman had imported from the West.

It is important to realize the gloomy surroundings in which these
gardens were planted. Public and private irresponsibility had turned
Poland from the great empire of the sixteenth century into one of the
sick states of Europe. Travellers remarked on the poverty and squalor
of the countryside—the French, too, on the absence of that symptom
of civilization, cheese[1]—and reported that roads and inns improved
once they crossed the border into Russia. It was, too, a landscape for
the most part poor in the natural accidents which were to become so
dear to the later, wilder English garden theorists like Richard Payne
Knight. The typical Polish country house stands in country which is
at best very slightly rolling, and only the occasional scarp at the edge
of a river valley gives some of the earliest landscape gardens a chance
of drama.

Like much of the art of the Enlightenment, these gardens were
made for a tiny group of well travelled aristocrats, the most important

[1] H. Vautrin, *L'Observateur en Pologne* (Paris, 1807), 167, relating to travels about 1782.

of them in fact closely related; one family tree of the Czartoryski and Poniatowski families embraces almost all of them (Text Fig. 1). From the first, their leaders called their landscape gardens "English."

> The master fancied he would take examples from nature:
> He ordered the digging of wolves' lairs and foxes' burrows...
> The deliberate felling of trees and sowing of all kinds of
> weeks ...
> His fantasy was that this was sort of English.[2]

But the more we look at them the more we find that what they were imitating were the *jardins anglais* of France.

This was in spite of the rising cultural prestige that England had begun to enjoy in eighteenth century Europe. Her agricultural reforms in particular were inspiring East European efforts to improve the state of the countryside, and in Russia at least these went hand in hand with landscape gardening.[3] The leaders of the little group I have mentioned went to England almost as often as to France; Izabella Czartoryska, for instance, celebrated her marriage by a trip in 1768 which took in both London and Paris, repeated this itinerary at much more leisure in 1772 to 1774, and followed her third Paris visit of 1787 with her third to England and first to Scotland in 1789–91;[4] her architect Zug was to write of Powązki that "Un voyage en Angleterre servit a développer les idées pleines de goût de cette Dame; elle revint, et les exécuta."[5] Her nephew Stanisław Kostka Potocki valued "Englishness" above all else; of his first garden at Olesin he wrote, "C'est ce qu'il y a de plus anglais en Pologne sans contreditte,"[6]

[2]   "Przywidziało się panu z natury brać wzory;
          Kazał pokopać wilcze jamy, lisie nory ...
          Drzewo zwalać umyślnie siać chwasty i zielska ...
          Miała to fantazyja być niby angielska."
F. Zabłocki, *Fircvk w zalotach* [The Dandy A-Wooing], a play written in 1781, quoted in J. Kott and S. Lorentz, *Warszawa wieku oświecienia* [Warsaw in the Century of the Enlightenment] (Warsaw, 1954).
[3] M. Ilyin, "Russian Parks of the Eighteenth Century," *Architectural Review*, 135 (1964), 100–111.
[4] H. Waniczkówna, "Izabella Czartoryska," *Polski Słownik Biograficzny* [Polish Biographical Dictionary], IV (Cracow, 1938), 241–246.
[5] C. C. L. Hirschfeld, *Théorie de l'art des jardins ... traduit de l'allemand* (the French edition), V (Leipzig, 1779–1785), 353; see note 12 below.
[6] Archiwum Główne Akt Dawnych (Warsaw), Archiwum Pałacowe Potockich, 262 I, Listy Hr. Stan. Potockiego do Małżonki od 1785 do 1790 r., 1 January 1787 (communicated by Agnieszka Morawińska).

THE CZARTORYSKIS AND THE PONIATOWSKIS

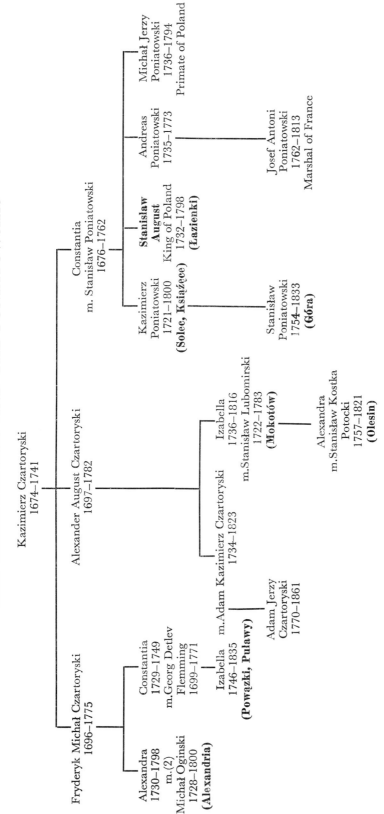

Names of the major gardens for which these patrons were responsible are in bold type in brackets.
Many relatives not significant for the purpose of this study are omitted.

TEXT FIG. 1

and of Ermenonville that "tout jolie qu'est la retraite de Rousseau, il ne faut pas la voire en revenant d'Angleterre."[7]

Of course, French influence was still all-pervading. The Polish aristocracy spoke French in preference to its native tongue; August Moszyński presented his essay on *le jardinage anglois* of 1774 to the King in French, and I am assured that Izabella Czartoryska's famous treatise of 1805 reads to a Pole as if a translation from the French. In 1761 her sister-in-law Izabella Lubomirska had commissioned palace plans from J. F. Coustou.[8] Closer to gardening, in 1774 Izabella Czartoryska brought to Poland with her the French painter J. P. Norblin, and installed him in one of the cottages of her garden at Powązki,[9] though his work in recording these gardens does not seem, unlike that of his contemporary Hubert Robert, to have extended to any real influence on their design. And since 1733, there had been the example of the emigré Leszczyński court at Nancy. But in my view what made the first Polish landscape gardens distinctly un-English was the use to which they were put.

In 1778 Archdeacon William Coxe stayed in Warsaw on his way to Russia. He had excellent introductions, and with his friends was invited to evening parties not only by the King at Łazienki, but also by the owners of two of the best new gardens, Kazimierz (Casimir) Poniatowski's Książęce to the south of Warsaw and Izabella Czartoryska's Powązki to the north.[10] At Książęce the guests arrived at nine in the evening, were led round the park, admired view and cascade, and then, "We passed through a subterraneous passage, long and winding, with here and there a single lamp, which shed a glimmering light; we came at length to a wooden door, which seemed the entrance to some hovel; it opened, and we found ourselves, to our great astonishment, in a superb saloon, illuminated with innumerable lamps. It was a rotunda, with an elegant dome of the most beautiful symmetry." We have Zug's plan for it (Fig. 1); there a splendid dinner was served, and music played in the concealed pas-

[7] *Loc. cit.*, 4 September 1787.

[8] S. Lorentz, "Z dziejów kształtowania się sztuki okresu Oświecenia w Polsce [the French summary is entitled "Influences françaises dans l'architecture polonaise au siècle des lumières"], *Biuletyn Historii Sztuki* [Bulletin of the History of Art], 23 (1961), 195–209.

[9] Z. Batowski, *Norblin* (Lwów, 1911); he was born in 1745, worked under Francesco Casanova de Seingalt, painted views of Powązki, Arkadia (see Fig. 9), and Puławy, and returned to France in 1804.

[10] W. Coxe, *Travels into Poland, Russia, Sweden and Denmark*, I (London, 1784), 175 and 178.

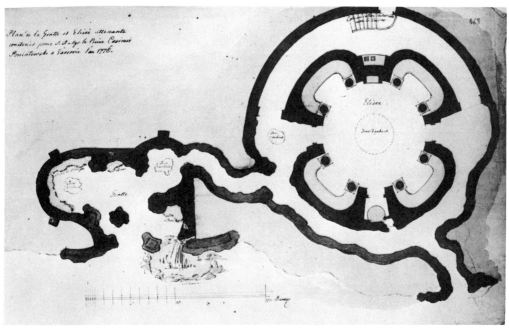

1. S. B. Zug, plan of grotto at Książęce, 1776 (Biblioteka Uniwersytecka w Warszawie, B.U.W.,
Inw. G.R. 137, photograph B.U.W.)

2. S. B. Zug, view of colonnade and mill at Solec, about 1772 (B.U.W., Inw. G.R. 146, photo: B.U.W.)

3. Lohrmann, view of Łazienki with Chinese arcades, about 1779 (photo: Instytut Sztuki, Polska Akademia Nauk)

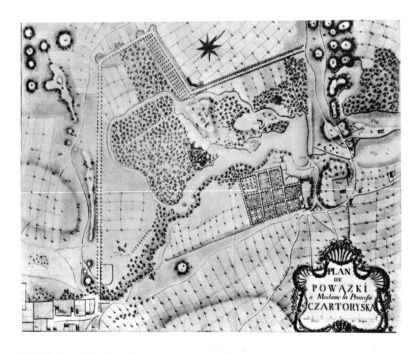

4. M. Żebrowski, plan of Powązki, about 1775 (taken from Ciołek, *Gärten in Polen*, by permission of Wydawnictwo "Arkady")

5. Z. Vogel, view of the Arch at Powązki, from a sketchbook, about 1794 (B.U.W., zbiory dawnego Uniwersytetu Warszawskiego, aneks 174, k. 2, photo: B.U.W.)

6. Z. Vogel, view of ruin at the end of Mokotów, about 1790 (B.U.W., zb. król. T. 175, nr. 232, photo by Ewa Kołowska-Tomczyk for I.S.P.A.N. supplied by B.U.W.)

7. Z. Vogel, view of Siedlce, about 1790 (photo: I.S.P.A.N.)

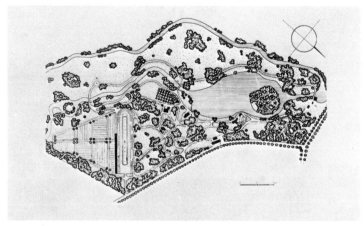

8. Plan of Arkadia, based by Gerard Ciołek on one of 1839,
(Ciołek, *Gärten in Polen*)

9. J.-P. Norblin, view of an arcade at Arkadia, 1789–90
(Muzeum Narodowe w Krakowie, Oddział Czartoryskich,
photo: I.S.P.A.N.)

10. Z. Vogel, view of the Great Bridge and Alexandra Potocka's house
at Olesin, 1789 (B.U.W., zb. król. T. 175, nr. 210; photo by Ewa
Kozłowska-Tomczyk for I.S.P.A.N. supplied by B.U.W.)

11. Arkadia, the Temple of Diana (photo: author, 1962)

12. Puławy, the Temple of the Sibyl (photo: author, 1962)

13. "Bridge adorned by a weeping Birch", from Izabella Czartoryska, *Myśli Rożne o sposobie zakładania ogrodów*, 1808 edition (photo: British Museum)

14. "Hidden boundary of a garden" from *Myśli Rożne* (as preceding)

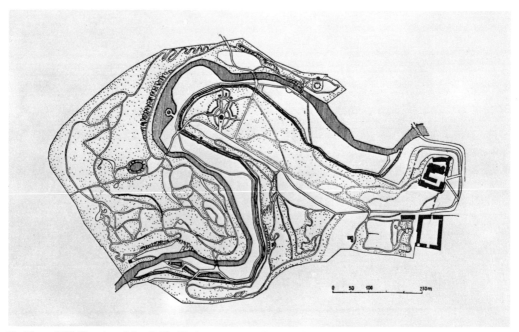

15. Plan of Vlašim, based by J. Krejčiřík on a map of the early nineteenth century. (taken from Dokoupil, *Historické Zahrady v Čechách a na Moravě* by permission of Nakladelství československých výtvarných umélců)

16. J. J. Wagner, the Temple of Love at Vlašim, from J. G. Grohmann, *Ideen-magazin für Liebhaber von Gärten*, IV (1802), cahier 45, no. 9 (photo: British Museum)

17. Krasný Dvůr, pavilion, about 1790 (photo: by Vladimir Hyhlik)

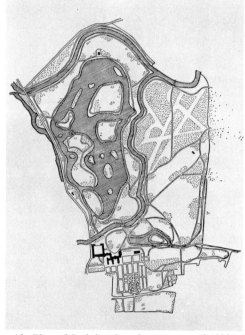

18. Plan of Lednice, based on a map of 1900 (from Dokoupil, *Historické zahrady*, as above)

19. Lednice, view from the minaret back to the house (photo: by Josef Ehm)

20. Lednice, the mill pond and the Temple of Apollo, 1817, by Kornhäusel (photo: by Josef Ehm)

sages. At Powązki they arrived for tea, upon a lawn "surrounded with large blocks of granite heaped one upon another, and fallen trees placed in the most natural and picturesque shapes," admired the cottages (where everyone seems to have been told how much it cost to line the bathroom with 3000 Meissen plaques at three ducats each) and the rustic bridges, sat on carpets under a "Turkish" tent, returned through the dusk to find the bridge "studded with several thousand lamps of different colours," took a cold supper in an open thatched pavilion, and after music and dancing left at two o'clock in the morning.

These were hardly English entertainments; they took place largely in the dark, they assumed the ground would be dry, and above all, they were essentially parties, not the long walks by people in ones, twos or threes we meet in contemporary English novels. Coxe was absolutely right to write of his last entertainments, "I can scarce form to myself a *fête champêtre* so elegant." The model for this use of a garden could only be the courtly life of Louis XVI's Versailles. Such a life was the ambition of the tiny circle around the King and his Czartoryski cousins.

There are scraps of evidence that one or two of these gardens— Mokotów, Puławy—had "wild promenades" created on their outer edges in or very soon after 1770, in association with work by the early neo-classical architect Efraim Schroeger.[11] But the first serious work was done after returning in 1772 from a journey to Italy by the Enlightenment's most original architect, Szymon Bogumił Zug.[12] The commission came from Kazimierz Poniatowski for a small estate at Solec south of Warsaw. It was costly—200,000 ducats, or £275,000 in English money of the time; never satisfactory, because the Vistula valley site was easily flooded; and, so far as we can tell from the surviving plan,[13] it remained an obvious attempt to break up a rec-

[11] See below pp. 108–110.

[12] For Zug's life and work see the new study by M. Kwiatkowski, *Szymon Bogumił Zug, Architekt Polskiego Oświecienia* [Szymon Bogumil Zug, Architect of the Polish Enlightenment] (Warsaw, 1971), which is the source for all information on his gardens not otherwise attributed. He was born at Merseburg in Saxony in 1733, came to Poland in 1756, and died there in 1807. In 1784 he wrote a brief but important account, already quoted, of the first twelve years of Polish landscape gardening which appeared in the French edition of Hirschfeld's *Theorie der Gartenkunst* (see note 5 above); the remarks which follow are also taken from it.

[13] Biblioteka Uniwersytetu Warszawskiego [Library of Warsaw University], Gabinet Rycin [Cabinet of Engravings], Inw. G. R. 117.

tangular site with a mound in the middle and to pepper it with "divers jolis morceaux" like a Gothic chapel. But Zug still felt proud of it twelve years later, as the gardens "furent les premiers de cette espèce à Varsovie, et consistent en fragments de jardins Anglois qu'on apprit alors à connoître ici." And we still have a splendid view of the end of the lake, with a very ragged looking mill and a great ruined colonnade that hid the existing house (Fig. 2). Gardens are very fragile, and we shall find how much we have to rely on plans and views for those ruined in war or over-run by suburban development.

Solec was laid out for Kazimierz, the King's elder brother; but the King, Stanisław August, was a patron with much more potential for the enthusiasts. He had a notorious passion for architecture, but for the first ten years after he came to the throne, in 1764, it was concentrated on the reconstruction of the great rambling Castle in the centre of Warsaw. He had, however, taken over the Lubomirskis' suburban house at Ujazdów, like Solec, south of the city, and in 1768 had begun to reshape it; that project was abandoned after the catastrophe of the First Partition in 1772. Later he had money only for modest experiments, and in 1774 we find his Italian architect, Merlini, putting up the first clearly neo-classical one, the 'Biały Domek', a cubical timber pavilion which recalls the designs of Gabriel.[14] So it was probably with the great Ujazdów park in mind that the amateur architect August Moszyński submitted to the King in January 1774 his *Essay sur le jardinage anglois*.[15] It exists only in manuscript, and, alas, the pocket at the back is empty that should hold the drawings that evidently represented the contribution by Zug to which the author refers (It is quite possible that they are now scattered in other Warsaw collections, and wrongly believed to be for his executed works). In fact the essay had very little effect on the park's development, which proceeded haphazard as Łazienski, the little bath-house on the lake, gradually became its centre; its designers kept straight avenues

[14] W. Tatarkiewicz, *Dominik Merlini* (Warsaw, 1955), 78.

[15] A. Morawińska, "Nieznany traktat Augusta Moszyńskiego o ogrodnictwie angielskim" [An unknown treatise by August Moszyński on English gardening], in J. Białostocki (ed.), *Myśl o sztuce i sztuka XVII i XVIII wieku* [Ideas about Art and Art in the 17th and 18th Centuries] (Warsaw, 1970), 255–328. Moszyński was born in 1732, married one of the Potockis, designed two churches near Tarnopol in the Ukraine, and died in 1783; T. Mańkowski, "August Moszyński, Architekt Polski XVIII Stulecia" [August Moszyński, a Polish Architect of the 18th Century], *Prace Komisji Historii Sztuki* [Work of the Commission for the History of Art], 4 (Warsaw, 1930), 169.

between its chief buildings, and their most interesting flirtation with
new ideas was a flimsy set of "Chinese" bridges designed by Kam-
setzer that from about 1775 to 1788 linked Łazienki on its island with
the lake shores to each side (Fig. 3).[16] We have to take the *Essay*
more as evidence of the way the pioneers thought than as influence
on those that followed them.

Moszyński was no enthusiast for fields that ran right up to the
windows of the country house; he still needed the baroque symmetrical approach and frame. Only on its far side would you reach the
English garden, with its streams, cascades, temples, its crenellated
ruined tower, its Philosopher's and Crusoe's huts, its skating pond,
and its inevitable artificial farm. In many ways this had not pro-
gressed very far from the late rococo garden, with its controlled plan
tricked out with fantastic structures; and, though Moszyński borrowed
from Whately, he himself said that he wanted to avoid the melancholy
which he believed the English to affect.

Disappointed in any hopes he may have had of commissions from
the King, Zug went on working for his family. In 1776 he started on
Książęce, the garden Archdeacon Coxe was to enjoy so much, again
for Kazimierz Poniatowski, and in 1779 on the adjoining Góra for
Kazimierz' son Stanisław. But these were both still rather constricted
sites, both had quite an axial underlying system, and both have vir-
tually disappeared, except for the remains at Góra of a "Masonic
Lodge" (Freemasonry turns up in some odd places in the Polish
Enlightenment, notably in the house and garden buildings at Dobrzyca
in Great Poland planned in 1798 by Zawadzki; Moszyński too was a
Mason). Zug left quite a detailed account of Książęce, and a shorter
one of Góra, in the essay published by Hirschfeld. Much more relaxed
was his work for two sisters-in-law, Izabella z Flemmingów Czartoryska at Powązki and Izabella z Czartoryskich Lubomirska at Mokotów.

Though something was under way at Powązki, on Warsaw's
northern outskirts, before Izabella went on her most ambitious journey
west, it seems to have taken shape mainly in a few years after her
return in 1774.[17] Its centre was a group of cottages on a small hill

[16] M. Kwiatkowski, "Łazienki 'w guście Chińskim'" [Łazienki 'in the Chinese taste'],
Biuletyn Historii Sztuki, 29 (1967), 171–190.

[17] M. Kwiatkowski, "Powązki," *Rocznik Warszawski* [Warsaw Yearbook], 9 (1969) 123–161.

(Fig. 4); from them views apparently radiated down to the lake—to the bridge, to various small ruins and houses, and through a triumphal arch to a fisherman's hut on a tiny island (Fig. 5).

At Mokotów, or *Mon Coteau*, serious work started in 1774.[18] The site was not really much better than Solec, another long rectangle cut out of the field system, but it must all have seemed much less artificial; Zug claimed for it "un aspect vraiement champêtre." The house kept its formal frame, but beyond that a maze of little paths wandered off into the bush; and when one emerged from it onto the shores of the lake one was in a new system of views, with a Chinese pavilion at the lake's head to the left (Fig. 6), ahead a chain of islands linked by bridges (Fig. 7), and to the right glimpses of the open country.[19]

In 1778, Zug started twenty years work on his most romantic commission of all, Arkadia, for a great friend of Izabella Czartoryska but, for once, not a relative—Helena Radziwiłłowa. It is forty odd miles west of Warsaw, near Łowicz, and to this it owes its survival; if far from absolutely intact, it is easily the best preserved Polish garden of the period (Fig. 8).[20] It has a planned framework of movement which unplanned later growth has partly obscured. From the entrance near the present kitchen garden, one should walk through a ruined arch between a Gothic cottage and Gothic arcades to the principal building, the Temple of Diana; from its portico one can see all the lake, with to the left its bridge disguised as an aqueduct and to the right an amphitheatre and an island which used to carry a monument (Fig. 9). From here there are two splendid walks, one all round the lake with views back to the Temple (Fig. 11), the other along the river beyond the aqueduct to a chapel and another island with a monument of 1790 that mimics that of Rousseau. There is no main house, and not much living accommodation, yet it is too far from

[18] M. Zakrzewska, "Mokotów. Pałacyk i założenie ogrodowe" [Mokotów. The little Palace and the garden lay-out]," *Kwartalnik Architektury i Urbanistyki* [Architecture and Urbanism Quarterly], 7 (1962), 45–70.

[19] A similar garden was that of Izabella Czartoryska's cousin Alexandra Ogińska at Siedlce; this used to be believed to date from the 1760's (e.g. by Gerard Ciołek, *Gärten in Polen* [Warsaw, 1954], 131), but the latest research puts it no earlier than 1783.

[20] J. Wegner, *Arkadia* (Łowicz, 1948); on the asymmetrical plan of the Temple and its position in the Picturesque movement, see also T. S. Jaroszewski, *Architektura doby Oświecenia w Polsce* [Architecture of the Age of Enlightenment in Poland] (Wrocław, Warsaw, Cracow, Gdańsk, 1971), 144.

Warsaw for large parties on the model of those at Powązki; here Helena Radziwiłłowa meditated alone in her temple, under the lines:

Oh! let me seek out some desolate shade
And there weep my sad bosom empty.

The place is full of such inscriptions, of the *triste et long regard;* it drips with the melancholy some of its forerunners had been so anxious to escape; it comes far closer than they to Ermenonville and to the more poetic English gardens. And from it Helena, calling herself the Vestal of Arkadia, carried on a long correspondence with Izabella, the Sybil of Puławy.

Before we reach Puławy, the grandest Polish landscape created before the Napoleonic Wars, we must introduce a more remarkable amateur than either Moszyński or the King, Stanisław Kostka Potocki. He was married to Izabella Lubomirska's daughter; on one of his many travels, David had made him the subject of one of the finest of Europe's equestrian portraits; and he had real ability as a designer. In 1776 he began the garden at Olesin, near Kurów and some seventy miles south-east of Warsaw, of which we have already heard him express his pride. We seem to have no surviving plan, only a dozen views by Zygmunt Vogel. It seems to have been a more modest Powązki; a small lake, two bridges one in stone and one in wood (Fig. 10), the owner's neat blocky classical pavilion and his wife's more romantic cottage, and a cascade that gushed through a ruinous arch. As his architect he had taken up Chrystian Piotr Aigner, the son of a carpenter in the service of the Czartoryskis at Puławy.[21] And it was Aigner to whom Izabella Czartoryska turned in the late 1780's when, becoming gradually more estranged from the Court in Warsaw, the Czartoryskis made Puławy their headquarters, and when the transfer was made final by the destruction of Powązki in the Prussian siege of Warsaw in 1794.

Puławy has a romantic site sixty miles south of Warsaw where the Vistula comes out of a cut through a low range of hills, leaving a steep scarp on each side of a broad flood plain. Here the designer

---

[21] T. S. Jaroszewski, *Chrystian Piotr Aigner*, Studia i materiały do teorii i historii architektury i urbanistyki [Studies and materials for the theory and history of architecture and urbanism], 5 (1965), 74–92, the chief source for my account of Puławy. Aigner was born in 1756, was sent to study in Rome, and began his Polish career in earnest in 1781; he lived on to restart it after 1815, and died in Italy in 1841.

could aim at the sort of effect that an English amateur of the Picturesque might recognize. The planting does not seem specially imaginative,[22] and the buildings are on the whole as one would expect, Chinese, Gothic and so on. But when you reach the Temple of the Sibyl (Fig. 12), built between 1798 and 1801 as a conventional version of the Roman Temple of Vesta, whose flight of steps and two lions face you benignly across the lawns in front of the house, you discover suddenly that it is perched on the edge of a cliff. The foundations on its far side are perhaps thirty feet high, and through a gap in the trees you can look down on an arm of the river and across the valley to the hills on its western side.

In pursuit of her enthusiasm for England, Izabella Czartoryska became, on her second visit, probably the first Polish magnate to recruit English garden experts. One, James Savage, became her head gardener at Puławy;[23] he does not seem to have done anything seriously to be called design, but when he died in 1816 she had a monument put up to him which says, in English:

> Here lies together with his son
> James Savage head gardner
> of the gardens at Puławy; his
> taste and his superior talents
> could only be compared to his
> probity and untained honesty.

Her other recruit was an Irishman, Denis McClear—to the Poles 'Mikler'—born in 1762, whose father had fled to Poland after the Irish risings of 1777.[24] He told people that he had learnt to design gardens in the service of the Duke of Bedford and under "the famous Legat."[25] He took years to learn the language and suffered some early disappointments, notably with Stanisław Poniatowski, Zug's patron

---

[22] I should add that I last visited it in 1962, when it needed some attention.

[23] T. S. Jaroszewski and J. Kowalczyk, "Artyści w Puławach w XVIII wieku" [Artists at Puławy in the 18th Century], *Biuletyn Historii Sztuki*, 21 (1959), 213–221.

[24] A. Przeździecki, *Podole, Wołyń, Ukraina, obrazy miejsc i czasów* [Podolia, Volhynia, Ukraine, Pictures of Places and Moments] II (Wilno, 1841), 126–141 (a whole chapter headed "Ogrody Miklera").

[25] I have so far been unable to check any of this career with British sources; McClear may well have been as big a liar as Charles Cameron. Any information that bears on his early years would be interesting.

at Góra, over a project at Korsuń.[26] But he discovered the *azalea pontica* in Polesie and planted it at Puławy; by 1800 he was the favoured designer of the magnates of eastern Poland, by then already Russian and now again incorporated in the Soviet Union. He was still at work when he died in 1840. His gardens are now, alas, destroyed or inaccessible; from Przeździecki's memoir we get a general vision of slow winding rivers and great trees; we are closer than ever to the Polish landscape.

Meanwhile Izabella Czartoryska had produced her own testament to the whole movement. It is a book, written about 1800 and published at Wrocław in 1805, called *Myśli Różne o sposobie zakładania ogrodów.*[27] It is a bit amateurish; half the text is taken up by details of the shapes and contents of different "clumps" (Fig. 13); there are lists of trees, many rather romantically engraved (Fig. 14), and a few pages about monuments and buildings; a brief exhortation to follow the needs and the character of the site is succeeded by a fifty-page catalogue of trees and plants. But even so, Izabella had come a long way from the artfully positioned entertainments of Powązki. The distortions of the French *jardin anglais* no longer obscured for Poles the sentiment and grandeur of the English Picturesque. After 1815, the second generation of the Enlightenment, like its contemporaries all over Europe, regarded the English taste in gardening as the norm. But it is specially poignant that the shift from court to country social life with which this went had been brought about through the destruction of Poland's political identity by her neighbours.

* * *

In Bohemia and Moravia—the Czech lands of the Hapsburg Empire—the Landscape Garden movement began more tentatively and

---

[26] In 1787 Stanisław Poniatowski had also built Poland's first full-size neo-Gothic country seat on the same site, ninety miles south of Kiev. The designs have been attributed to one Jan Lindsay (born in Poland, 1759–1822), but it is tempting to connect them with J. H. Müntz (1727–1798) who drew Gothic and Moorish buildings at Kew for Chambers and who laid out an earlier garden, of which we have no description, at Korsuń in 1782; Jaroszewski, *Architektura doby Oświecienia w Polsce*, 190; Alistair Rowan, *Garden Buildings*, RIBA Drawings Series (London, 1968), 36 (showing a 'Moorish' pavilion); Sandra Wedgwood, entry on this drawing in a forthcoming volume (L–N) of the RIBA *Drawings Catalogue.*

[27] C. Krassowski, "Nowatorstwo 'Myśli' Izabeli Czartoryskiej" [The Innovations of Izabella Czartoryska's 'Ideas'], *Biuletyn Historii Sztuki*, 27 (1965), 227–230.

never triumphed so completely as it did in Poland. Nor, for that matter, has it been so much studied. The reasons are related. The Czech Baroque exerted as vigorous a hold on builders in the eighteenth century as it does on art historians in the twentieth; the neoclassicism which succeeded it has seemed by comparison insipid, indecisive, and, to the Czech historian, an alien manner to boot, for under Joseph II the Enlightenment meant not a national revival, as in Poland, but growing centralization on Vienna.

It was possible to believe that Bohemia might have provided fertile ground for the new garden ideas, because of the wildness and roughness with which the Baroque sometimes experimented, most remarkably in Count Špork's extraordinary hermitage or "Bethlehem" of 1717 at Kuks. But the gap in time is far too long. The first descriptions of anything that might qualify as landscape date from about 1770, and they are none too convincing. By 1769, the now lost garden at Červený Dvůr (Rothenhof), in the south of Bohemia a few miles west of Krumlov, possessed a grotto, a lake with an island and a little bridge, and Chinese and Dutch pavilions; but the one view we possess, apparently of the same period, shows a very big formal lay-out in which one corner is perhaps a little ragged.[28] In September 1770 the extravagant Count Albert von Hoditz entertained Frederick the Great at his new garden at Rosswald or Rudoltice, in "Czech Silesia."[29] The guests came early, and spent much of the morning passing through a Shepherds' Festival in Arcady, one moment surrounded by dancers and musicians, another offering incense at a Druid altar, another accompanied on the lake by the local girls as so many swimming naiads. The early landscape furniture was there, the grottos and waterfalls and pagodas and the fancy dairy. But what is very clear is that this was a rococo entertainment, elaborately rehearsed by the talented Count's big household; and as we look closer we see that it happened in a rococo garden too, for in what real landscape garden would Apollo have presided in a Hesperidean garden of clipped cedars?

The first major landscape garden of which we are well provided with views and plans is that of the Auerspergs at Vlašim, forty miles

---

[28] Practically all the information in this section is taken from Z. Dokoupil, P. Naumann, D. Riedl, and I. Veselý, *Historické zahrady v Čechách a na Moravě* [Historical Gardens in Bohemia and Moravia] (Prague, 1957), checked against Z. Wirth (ed.), *Umělecké Památky Čech* [Artistic Monuments of Bohemia] (Prague, 1957).

[29] P. Drechsler, *Albert von Hoditz, der Wundergraf von Rosswald* (Leobschütz, 1895), 53–72.

south-east of Prague. We know that work of some kind started in 1755, and in time it took in a winding mile of river and steep-sided valley (Fig. 15). Our views, however, date from 1802 to 1805.[30] They show as an open domed temple, on a tiny round island (Fig. 16), an astonishingly mad Chinese pavilion whose ground floor was open and whose upper floor was reached by a curious bridge from a separate stair turret, a Bards' Grove, grottos, inscriptions, and so forth. But they do not show us a garden that has been there for long; the trees are still young, the formal clearings neat. The whole scheme is very reminiscent of the extensions which we know were made in the 1790's to the great garden of the archbishops of Olomouc at Kroměříž in Moravia. Here, too, the open Temple of Friendship sat on a rocky island, and a two-storey Chinese pavilion was reached by an outside stair.

Kroměříž (Kremsier) kept its main Baroque layout all this time, and only in the 1830's was it swept away.[31] At Nové Hrady, on the Austrian border south-east of České Budějovice, the Buquoys only added an Arcadian Village to their existing park; their bathing place, the *Terezino údolí* (Teresa's dell) with an artificial waterfall, lay separate from it like a hermitage. Elsewhere landscape lay-outs preserved, or even deliberately included, a few of the great formal vistas that had pleased the previous generation. An example is that made before 1788 by the "court gardener" Födisch for the Černíns at Krasný Dvůr (Schönhof) thirty miles east of Karlovy Vary; its Doric temple and Gothic octagonal monument and exquisite banded classical summer-house (Fig. 17) dot the woods on each side of an avenue that leads to an obelisk of 1801.[32]

The first magnate to have a convincing landscape made for him was Count Jan Rudolf Chotek, a leading Minister of the Vienna government, who became *Oberstburggraf* of Bohemia in 1802, and who

---

[30] A. Pucherna and V. Berger, *Der Fürstlich Auersbergische Park zu Wlaschim in Böhmen* (1805); The Bard's Grove and the Temple of Love in the middle distance of their main view also appear in Johann Gottfried Grohmann, *Ideenmagazin für Liebhaber von Gärten*, IV (Leipzig, 1802), Cahier 44, no. 8 and Cahier 45, no. 9 (see illustration 16).

[31] O. Kuča, "Zámecké zahrady v Kroměříži" [The Castle Gardens at Kroměříž], *Umění* [Art], 6 (Prague, Československá Akademie Věd, Kabinet Theorie a Dějin Umění, 1958), 312–388.

[32] Z. Wirth and J. Benda, *Castles and Mansions* (Prague, 1955), 286, says the park was laid out in 1781–1783; Grohmann, *Ideenmagazin*, illustrates an Ionic temple by a cascade (III, Cahier 35, no. 7); a round temple on a hill (III, Cahier 36, no. 8); and the Gothic temple or monument (IV, Cahier 37, no. 8).

was responsible for the first gardens on the hillside of Letná which overlooks Prague. In 1784, he started work on the park at Veltrusy, on the Vltava about 20 miles downstream from Prague,[33] with the diversion of the river. The sweep of its old course became a sickle-shaped belt of trees, and in this we find a chain of small buildings and monuments. At the west end a neat square pavilion on a bridge was built in 1797 in memory of Field Marshal Laudon;[34] in the southern angle lies the prettiest group, the Temple of Friendship of 1792–94 and the Doric Temple of 1811, with a grotto between them; in the northern stretch there is an Egyptian Pavilion of 1816–19, and beyond it, in an oval clearing, the Maria Teresa pavilion of 1811–13; there are monuments to garden experts, Hirschfeld and the Viennese Richard van der Schotten. Although it saw some big parties, like the visit of Francis I in 1820, it looks like a garden for reflective walks.

Yet even Chotek would not shake the old Baroque methods off. From 1802 to 1822 J. F. Jöndl was building him a great neo-classical house, to the designs of the Dresden architect Schuricht (who provided a lot of the designs engraved by Hirschfeld and by Grohmann in his *Ideen-Magazin für Liebhaber von Gärten*), at Kačina, east of Kutná Hora; before building started he was directing the planting himself, with suggestions from one of the Jacquins, keepers of the Viennese botanical garden.[35] He was modern enough to bring grass and trees right up to the walls of the house, but from it he laid out great radiating avenues—one of them continued on the far side of the lake—and woods and groves with star plans. As late as 1820 the Rohans at Sychrov were content with paths that meandered across and between two great diverging vistas. At Lednice in Moravia, Alois Josef von Liechtenstein built in 1794 a Temple of the Sun at the centre of his park's radiating alleys. There were no Hubert Roberts here, recording with enthusiasm on canvas the destruction of the formality that had existed before.

[33] O. Špecinger, *Chotkovské Veltrusy* (Prague and Kralupy, 1957).

[34] Laudon's admirers included more than one garden romantic. At Hadersdorf in Austria the whole park was adorned with trophies in his honour, culminating in a monument of 1790, set in "durch Verwilderung der Gegend selbst herbeigeführten Stimmung"; Renate Wagner-Rieger, *Wiens Architektur im 19. Jahrhundert* (Vienna, 1970), 69.

[35] L. Macková, *Zámek Kačina*, Nové prameny 2 (Prague, 1956). M. Šipr, *Zámecký areál Lednice—Valtice* (n.p., n.d.); biographical notes on Hardtmuth and Kornhäusel; Carl Höss, *Fürst Johann II von Liechtenstein und die bildende Kunst* (Vienna, 1908).

But at Lednice (Eisgrub) before his death in 1805 Alois Josef had entrusted Fanti and van der Schotten with the start of the most ambitious landscape project in the Czech lands.[36] Its first major structure was already built, at huge effort and expense—a 200-foot minaret of 1797 by Josef Hardtmuth out in the marshes of the river Dyje. Between 1805 and 1811, under Alois Josef's brother Johann I, the whole area between this and the house was turned into a picturesque lake dotted with wooded islands (Fig. 18), so that from the minaret back to the house you look across six alternating bands of land and water (Fig. 19). In 1807, Hardtmuth built the Hansenburg, a sizeable house camouflaged as a Gothic ruin, on the river's far bank. Then an avenue was created to link Lednice with the family's other great house at Valtice (Feldsberg) right on the Austrian border, five miles away. It made the three mile chain of mill ponds part of the park, and from 1817 Josef Kornhäusel's Temple of Apollo presided over one end of them (Fig. 20). To the south-east, the Temple of Diana or *Rendezvous* went up to Hardtmuth's designs in 1810, a hunting lodge in the shape of a huge Roman triumphal arch, and further into the woods Kornhäusel built the great colonnade of 1817 which is a monument to Johann I's father and brothers. Lednice was only fifty miles from Vienna, and the family kept on rebuilding; the big remodelling of the house by Wingelmüller, in a manner reputed to be predominantly English Gothic, brought with it in 1845 a splendid iron and glass Palm House, the first of its kind in the Austrian Empire, by the English designer P. H. Desvignes. After Wilhelm Larche became the new head of the gardens in 1859 he laid out the vast formal flower gardens that exist today, and which it is interesting to see a contemporary describe as "setting the house free," presumably from the park's big encroaching trees.

The English feeling that the Poles had captured so quickly only really seems to reach Bohemia well into the nineteenth century. One of the prettiest smaller parks is that at Ratibořice, near Náchod on the Silesian border.[37] It was begun in 1811 by Wilhelmine von Sagan, who was daughter of the Duchess of Courland who had been Talleyrand's mistress, and who had spent several years in Warsaw after 1790 in close contact with the Czartoryskis and the Potockis; in this unadorned retreat she received her lover Metternich while the conferences

---

[37] Z. Wirth, *Ratibořice* (Prague, 1956).

went on that created the last grand alliance against Napoleon. If there is one thing that the makers of the early Bohemian landscape gardens have in common, it is their close contact with the Viennese court; they are outlying members of a movement that had started earlier in Austria, with Field Marshal Count Lacy's works of the 1760's at Neuwaldegg, and which by 1790 was fully established there.[38] But, as I have said in explaining the historians' lack of interest in them, this was the time when the Czech lands most lacked a creative culture of their own.

BIBLIOGRAPHICAL NOTE

Although it is ill arranged and much of its information has been superseded, Gerard Ciołek's big *Ogrody w Polsce* (1952)—I have used the German version, *Gärten in Polen* (1954)—is a great inspiration to all students of Polish gardens. Among its children is the series *Rejestr Ogrodów Polskich* which began to appear in 1964 but has not so far added to our knowledge of the major gardens mentioned in this essay; future instalments may well do so. Very useful check-lists are provided by Stanisław Łoza, *Architekci i Budowniczowie w Polsce* (1954) and Jerzy Łoziński and Adam Miłobędzki, *Atlas Zabytków Architektury w Polsce* (1967).

I cannot emphasize too much how great my debt is to Agnieszka Morawińska for her kindness in sharing freely with me her knowledge of Polish gardens and of their cultural background. I am sorry that I cannot make a similar acknowledgement in respect of Czechoslovakia.

[38] Wagner-Rieger, *Wiens Architektur*, 68–73.

Conclusions

Nikolaus Pevsner

$\mathbf{W}$e are all historians here, those who spoke, opening their arsenals of data and letting us participate in the results of their research, and those who contributed to the discussion. Now, since I had nothing to offer in the field and am a mere chairman, let me tell you in conclusion of this colloquium how I got interested in the English eighteenth century Picturesque and what value in my opinion this not so usual approach may have.

Some time after the beginning of the Second World War the *Architectural Review* lost its principal editor J. M. Richards (now Sir James Richards) to the Ministry of Information. He suggested me as his—temporary—successor and moved to Cairo. I did what I could, and this would have been entirely in matters of contemporary building, if it had not been for the co-owner of the *Review*, H. de Cronin Hastings. He is a brilliant man who likes to stay in the background. He had read Christopher Hussey's *The Picturesque*, the great classic of the movement. It is to Christopher Hussey that we shall dedicate the printed version of this colloquium. I also had of course read the book—even several years before I settled down in England, but purely as a piece of English art history. It was de Cronin Hastings who dropped a remark in his studiedly casual way indicating that surely Hussey's *Picturesque* and our day-to-day work for the *Review* were really one and the same thing. This is what set me off. With de Cronin's blessing I started on a book whose subject was just this aside of the great pathfinder. In the end the book was never written, and instead only a few papers on the Georgian Picturesque came out, all but one in the *Review* (1944–8), and one which was the longest and went into

119

the *Art Bulletin* (1949). As my thought in these years developed. I realised that the missing link between the Picturesque and twentieth-century architecture was the picturesque theory chiefly of Uvedale Price, but also of Payne Knight and Repton, and even Reynolds.

Price's categories are Variety, Intricacy, Irregularity, Contrast, Surprise, Irritation and Accident. Of these Reynolds in his Discourse of 1786 had the first three and the last. But whereas Price applies his categories to landscape, Reynolds uses them for arguing about townscape. He prefers the accidents of town growth to the regularity of town planning which latter, he said, can easily lead to weariness. Nor does Reynolds exclude Wren's plan for London from his censure.

Now if you think of the situation of architecture in the twentieth century, it is a familiar fact that twentieth century architecture was created in opposition against Beaux-Arts composition, or in Central Europe against the neo-Baroque and in England against the Wrenaissance. The Beaux-Arts, the Wrenaissance and the neo-Baroque all went in for symmetry and hence no surprise nor any irregularity.

But the new style was more than the introduction of new elements of form and compositional principles. Architects such as Gropius—think of the Bauhaus building—laid it down that to create a successful building, i.e. a building which functions well, the architect must start from an investigation of the function of his building getting down to such details as the production lines in a factory, the movement lines in a hospital and so on. Once this process is accepted as the basic necessity of architecture, then it will come as no surprise to anyone that the result of the process can only very rarely be symmetrical. Instead the architect has to start from an asymmetrical group and convert it into something aesthetically valuable. This applies to town planning as much as to individual buildings. In town-planning Camillo Sitte in 1889 had analyzed medieval towns and their details as the very opposite of Versailles or Karlsruhe planning, and Sir Raymond Unwin had refined Sitte in applying his doctrine to the situation to-day. In his best estate, the Hampstead Garden Suburb in London, begun in 1907, he combined Picturesque planning with a few main axial roads planned straight.

As for the individual building, you can almost pick any recent compositionally complex group at random, and you will find variety, intricacy, contrasts. The late Walter Gropius's Bauhaus of 1925–6 I have already mentioned. In England the new universities are the best example and the Greater London Council's housing schemes, notably Roehampton. Public housing in the United States lags behind, and this is one reason why over here I try always to preach the application of Visual Planning principles instead of the pernicious gibberish of sociological planning.

My examples, you will have noticed, are not up-to-the-minute. But if you now take more recent architecture, the style has certainly changed from Falling Water to Paul Rudolph and the Boston City Hall—and the change does not please me—but whatever the value of the new formal elements, genuine or gimmicks, the principles of Uvedale Price still hold sway.

Here, in my opinion, what the landscape section of Dumbarton Oaks is doing could assume a new significance.